T0096456

Being in Every Moment of our Life
Alain Duhayon

Spiritual Practice and Daily Life's Collection

The aim of this collection of essays is to bring together themes that were developed during lectures and teaching sessions. These teachings respond to the questions of practitioners who encountered obstacles, in their daily life, and in their practice.

Although these themes are approached in a Buddhist framework, they may also be of interest to anyone seeking responses to the difficulties of daily life in a turbulent modern world.

The first book in this collection "Petits galets sur le chemin" [Small Peebles on the Path, not translated into English], provided an overview of a path by answering questions asked by both beginners and experienced practitioners.

Petits galets sur le chemin, ["Small Peebles on the Path", not translated into English], Alain Duhayon, 2013

Being in Every Moment of our Life

Alain Duhayon

Translated by Marie Barincou
and Karuna Fenner

RABSEL
PUBLICATIONS

ORIGINAL TITLE : ÊTRE, EN CHAQUE INSTANT DE NOTRE VIE, Rabsel Éditions, 2019

RABSEL PUBLICATIONS
16, rue de Babylone
76430 La Remuée, France
www.rabsel.com
contact@rabsel.com

© Rabsel Publications, La Remuée, France, 2023

ISBN 978-2-36017-049-4

Table of Contents

Homage

Through a breath, appearances, and sensations; what to wish for, and remember that happiness is the manifestation of appearances, the richness of the mind in its nature?

Wanting to remember and remembering, in the spring and fall of each practice, every day,

Using methods and supports to remember but, above all, remembering,

Loving to remember and remembering to love,

Bringing together the practices, the aspirations, the intentions to remember and reminders of love, with all that we are ready to give,

Giving oneself by remembering and to remember by the giving of oneself,

The more arid life is, the more it needs moisture,

The tears of compassion and of love, the dew of happiness, the rain of giving,

When the ego starts perspiring a little moisture, sooner or later the storm arrives to end this aridity,

Remembering, this is the condition for the excess to fall into us,

All excesses are linked to the lack of remembering,

When we truly understand the meaning of remembering, we will know that it is presence, and that presence is enlightenment.

To Karmapa, to Kalu Rinpoche and above all to Lama Teunsang[1], who has always been my torch in the night.

---

1   Translator's note, Venerable Lama Teunsang is Montchardon spiritual guide. Montchardon, "*The unchanging garden of activity*", is a Buddhist centre located in France within the Karma Kagyu tradition of Tibetan Buddhism.

A caution

This book aims to highlight my observations as a spiritual counsellor over many years of how people function and can heal and grow.

I discuss the mindset with which we approach the various aspects of our existence. I also give directions about how to reduce the negative effects of our sequential way of living our daily life.

While I have been a practitioner and teacher for many years, I don't detail practices in this book. These will be the subject of other books.

In fact, the various topics covered deserve theoretical and practical treatments by fully qualified teachers.

Here, I limit myself to sketching out the meaning of a unified vision of the different moments of our existence.

For people in search of meaning, whether they are beginners or already making progress on the path, this global vision makes it possible to move to a more harmonious way of living by practicing different methods.

This book, derived from public teachings, intentionally keep a little of the oral flavor to support integration. Thus, for the reader as for the listener, integration requires vigilant attention, repetition, time, and aspiration. It is useful to read this book several times, chapter by chapter.

Introduction

The current interest in meditative practices can sometimes seem like a superficial response to selfish and egocentric needs.

Therefore, it is useful to place these practices into their context, that is to say within an authentic spiritual process. The profound meaning of this spiritual process can be very open. It is not based on dogma but relies on concrete principles.

These principles are not objects of belief. They must be experienced. They are as valid for modern life as they were, 2500 years ago, when the Buddha first expressed them.

After all, what difference is there between the Buddha and us? He recognized the nature of his mind while we haven't.

We must naturally exercise doubt: the doubt that leads us to experiment, not the skeptical doubt that prevents us from doing so.

Meditating without understanding the ultimate meaning of this practice can lead us to think of meditation as a de-stressing technique rather than a way to solve the fundamental problem of the ego.

When the basis of our difficulties and sufferings is not defined, we may continue to see the cause of our problems in our circumstances, or in others, without solving anything.

Therefore, it is vital that we remember the principles on which our spiritual practice needs to be based.

Spiritual practice assumes that we remember our sense of self in its natural essence and where it comes from, pure awareness. It also requires that we remember that all living beings have the same natural essence.

For balance and peace to be established, equanimity between the individual sense of self and the manifest world is essential, as is remembering its fundamental nature.

Ignorance and ego grasping

Fundamental ignorance

The Buddha points to the veiled state of the mind as the root cause of suffering from beginningless time. From this state of ignorance, duality arises in every moment.

This is the reason why the Buddha taught the need to establish a state of awareness—presence to immediacy—to remove the cause of suffering and, consequently, the chain of interactions which results from ignorance.

Careful observation demonstrates our state of ignorance, an absence of awareness, which is always at play in everyone.

Dualistic grasping

In our veiled state of mind, what perceives is grasped as "me", and what is perceived, the phenomenal world, is grasped as "other", which means distinct from the perceiver, the "me". These two—that which perceives and that which is perceived—are grasped from their appearance.

This arbitrary grasping of an "I" or "me" and an "other" entails the grasping of a third, which is the division or separation between these two. For the "I", the reality of this separation seems to be proven by the appearance, the surface of the perceived phenomena.

Dividing the field of awareness from awareness itself is suffering. This division is also incoherent. When we abide within the field of awareness as a field of space, there is neither interruption nor obstruction, just like a bubble. Choosing to focus on separation is only random.

When a child makes a bubble by dipping a small ring in liquid soap, the space in which this bubble is produced is a unified field; there is no inside or outside in this field.

When the child produces it, the field in which the bubble forms remains as it is, unchanged, just as awareness remains unchanged in observing phenomena.

Why, then, do we identify ourselves as the space within the bubble? In this reductive identification, we perceive the bubble's inner space [ourselves] as being absolutely distinct from the outer space [the world], when actually space is undifferentiated.

Why do we absolutely grasp an interior as being "me" and an exterior as being "other", when they are the same? Particularly as the film of soap defining the bubble is only a limit in air, and not a limit in space itself.

Why don't we see and acknowledge that from the point of view of space itself there is an abiding unity? It is only from the perspective of gross appearances that a relative distinction between inside and outside can be made.

The observing child perceives the space within the bubble as being distinct from the space outside the bubble. As an infant, the child is caught up in the play of appearances. Whereas the adult knows that the space within which a bubble forms, that exists and disappears is undifferentiated.

Cognitive grasping

This same confusion operates whenever our experience of awareness is limited by the surface appearance of phenomena. This confusion propels us to grasp at the play of appearances. We relate to our bodily envelope as "me" and to the exterior, or external object, as "other". From then on, this grasping at appearances produces the experience of division in everything we perceive.

When we actually observe how the ego operates, this division seems absurd. The ego grasps an external object and identifies with it.

This is called the "domain of ego extension". We can observe this with a nightmare. We might be pursued by a monster, feel afraid and run away from it, often by waking up. And what do we say then? "I was chased by a monster"!

This demonstrates that, awake or asleep, we identify with a self who is pursued, and create a monster that is distinct from us, and which pursues us. Here again, we experience division. Yet the very same mind, and the very same consciousness has produced this absurdity, the idea of a "me". It is the same mind that produced the monster, the pursuit, being chased, as well as the context in which that pursuit happened.

On top of the grasping of the appearance of an object of perception, we are adding another aberration by associating a name to a form. Whether an object is exterior—like a material object—or interior—like a thought—we think we know them, absolutely, by naming them. A name can't capture a whole object, and what constitutes it. Rather it only points to a surface, or an appearance. We consider objects to be units that exist independently in themselves when in fact they are composed and depend on other things.

As a result, we confuse "savoir" [knowledge] with "connaissance" [understanding, awareness, and lived experience]. Knowledge is limited to the appearance and solidifies phenomena in time and space. Awareness and lived experience on the other hand, remain forever within the immediacy of the moment.

This confusion between knowledge and awareness impoverishes and impedes our immediate experience. It interrupts the harmonious equanimity between the individual and its surrounding world.

The domination of knowledge over those who do not "know" led, for example, Christopher Columbus to discover America when he thought he had discovered India. Following his assumption, natives were then called "Indians". Thinking he knew, Christopher Columbus started dominating indigenous people who knew their land better. Many other examples of colonialism illustrate this point.

Thinking that knowledge is sufficient is what often prevents a practitioner from implementing and applying meditative instructions.

Cognitive grasping is characterized by the fact that we perceive each of these three, self, other and division, or if you will, an interior, exterior and division, as having an absolute existence, a real existence as such. We consider these to be independent units, not composed of parts, with an intrinsic existence, that is to say, not dependent on any cause. This is indefensible[2].

The three spheres

Me, other and division or, subject, object and division are called in Buddhist teachings, "the three spheres".

Seeing each of these three spheres as uncompounded units implies that they are eternal, not subject to change, which is obviously wrong.

Considering that the I, other and division could have an intrinsic existence would be like believing that the bubble, in the above analogy, always existed, without any cause that produced it, which is absurd.

The self, a dependency system

The notion of "me" arises from grasping at another. This dependency on the object of perception is the basis of all dependencies. In meditation practice, for example, it leads practitioners to maintain a mental activity, through which we feel that we

2   Translator's note, the most decisive arguments in Buddhist philosophy show-ing that the self and phenomena lack an absolute existence can be found in "*Nagarjuna's Middle Way, Mulamadhyamakakarika*". Chapter I and XV. Translated by Mark Siderits and Shoryu Katsura, Wisdom Publications, 2013, Boston.

exist. Therefore, we comment, reflect, and analyze, in order to talk and think about things, even about thoughts themselves, rather than letting mental activity dissolve.

Aristotle said, "nature abhors a vacuum", similarly the ego itself, when noticing the absence of an object or a phenomenon to identify with, feels threatened by what is perceived as a nothingness.

Depending as we are on internal or external phenomena, we don't take the opportunity to experience a real sense of being.

It is in fact, in meditation practice, that we can experience a real feeling of being, a feeling of being that doesn't depend upon the gaze of others, nor on social engagements (without in any way devaluing these).

Of course, other practices can also lead to this actualization of a real feeling of being that is free from dependency, such as deep relaxation or Kum Nyé (Tibetan yoga).

The self therefore exists in dependence on phenomena, in fact, on all phenomena, whether gross, material, external, subtle, or interior, including thoughts, sensations, and emotions.

In general, the functioning of the ego is based on three modes, traditionally called the "three poisons": attraction for what is pleasant; repulsion towards what is unpleasant or challenging; indifference and ignorance towards what seems neither pleasant nor unpleasant.

However, as inconsistency is the realm of the ego, this functioning, although simple at first, generates complications. When, for example, we get into the habit of being unwell or restless, it becomes a structure that the ego cannot easily live without. The habit feeds a very powerful thirst that takes us back to that state however negative and unpleasant this state is; in the same way that an alcoholic goes back to his bottle, or an addict goes back to the substance he or she is addicted to.

This functioning of the ego is the unique basis of all dependencies. The dualistic mind, which is ignorant of its own nature, is reduced to what in the West is called, "the conscious". The dualistic mind seeks unity through fusion with objects of perception, gross or subtle, which are impermanent. Trapped in seeking, unity is never achieved. This perpetuates constant frustration and unsatiated thirst.

Our need for reassurance, well-being, and unity, lead us into a whole range of addictions such as drugs, sports, the internet, smartphones, work and restlessness. However, none of these relatively existing objects can remove the fundamental feeling of separation from our true nature.

The division that the ego creates between self and other is reflected in our self through our use of distinctions such as conscious and unconscious, high and low, masculine and feminine.

Domain of ego extension

The grasping of phenomenal appearances and a self that arises grasped in dependence on another is a basis for the notion of an owner, a subject who appropriates phenomena. This appropriation is exercised in a random way, independently of whether an object of perception is interior, like a thought, or exterior, like a place.

As soon as there is a self, there is another. When there is a me, there is mine and as soon as there is another, there is yours.

We should remember that our self, other, division, mine and yours and the division between them are arbitrary and subject to change.

The propensity to impute ownership and property, whether it be "her hospital room" or "my table" in a restaurant, leads us to claim a sense of ownership, even if we are in a place for the very first time.

The ideas of territory and ownership are ubiquitous. We apply them even when we don't "own" an object, an idea, a place as such. Consequently, any incursion that seems to question "our property", our subjective notion of possessiveness, triggers conditioned reactions of unconscious tendencies and disturbing emotions: ignorance, desire-attachment, anger-aversion, pride, and jealousy.

We should acknowledge that this idea of ownership is subjective, and that the notion of owner leads to the production of disturbing emotions and suffering no matter what the triggering phenomenon is.

Fundamental or habitual tendencies

To sum up, dualistic grasping at an ego arises from fundamental ignorance. Cognitive grasping ascribes an absolute existence to the self, the other, and to the division between them. These three, which are called "the three spheres", are each then perceived as unified, uncompounded, and intrinsically existent.

This fundamental separation is experienced as suffering, as a loss of unity, a lost paradise. This suffering will be experienced recurrently throughout our individual existence, in every experience of separation, including the smallest, which happen constantly in daily life and also within our spiritual practice.

We are largely unaware of the unbearable suffering in fundamental separation. It is largely unconscious and reenergized through each experience of separation in our life. The separation produces psycho-physical reactivity that manifest as the play of our fundamental energetic tendency. This play also conceals our suffering, which contributes further to our fundamental state of ignorance.

The ego is a bounded territory that ignores its arbitrary and illusory nature. To survive situations of suffering, the ego adopts a strong positional reaction towards what it considers to be other. These reactions arise from dualistic grasping. This is largely unconscious, difficult to observe, and even harder to control. However, we can observe through the characteristics of the play of unconscious tendencies that appear to the so called "conscious" dimension of the mind.

In Tibetan Buddhism, the illusory aspect of our functioning is called "Namshé". The way the ego responds to separation come in five forms[3]. Ignorance, desire-attachment, anger-aversion, pride, and jealousy.

Through meditation, a practitioner returns to unity by realizing the essence of these negative tendencies. In meditation, these energetic tendencies are experienced as the natural wisdom of the mind, which has five aspects: the all-pervading wisdom, discriminating wisdom of love, mirror-like wisdom, wisdom of equanimity and all- accomplishment wisdom.

In the state of duality, our mind is dominated by one of the five energetic tendencies, even though

---

3   In the Tantric context, the five forms are linked to the notion of the five families, which relate to the five aspects of wisdom called "Dhyani Buddha". Each family and wisdom have a name:
- "Buddha", for ignorance.
- "Padma", for desire-attachment.
- "Vajra", for anger-aversion.
- "Ratna", for pride.
- "Karma", for jealousy.

all of them are at work. However, our dominant energetic tendency is the one that arises most often when there is conflict with, or separation from, the outside world, but also in regard to any arising mental phenomena.

It is therefore important for practitioners to know which energetic tendency dominates their mind, the family they belong to, the one to which they are most closely aligned with. Once we know our dominant negative tendency, we consequently know the wisdom quality we are related to. We should also learn to recognize the energetic tendencies of all the other families as they arise in concert with each other.

The ego has difficulty approaching the play of these tendencies because its own mode of operating is to solidify relative reality by categorizing everything through the imposition of names and forms. This is what is meant by conceptual grasping.

When practitioners observe themselves through the time and space of their daily life, they can recognize the play of their tendencies through the recurring patterns in their behavior. However, it isn't sufficient to simply observe tendencies in daily life. In order to make deeper progress, we need to become aware of the essence of the phenomena that are tied to our tendencies. This is developed in the immediacy of meditation practice.

Without fundamental ignorance, the energetic tendencies cannot exist. Still, there is no such thing as an intrinsically existing person with energetic tendencies, such as anger and the other four tendencies. There has never been, is not and never will be such a person. In the same way that there is no such thing as an intrinsically existing clay pot. Such a pot never was, is not and never will be.

A clay pot is composed of the interdependent elements of space, clay, water, fire, and air. Likewise, the energetic tendencies do not exist independently of each other. They are all present even when one dominates.

In its ignorance, the ego grasps at everything, including itself, projecting that they are all composed of uncompounded parts.

In other words, fundamental ignorance is the cause of dualistic grasping. This grasping entails the pain of separation. This suffering and this separation engender the manifestation of five energies or tendencies[4] : ignorance, desire-attachment, anger-aversion, pride, and jealousy.

We shouldn't put ourselves or others in boxes regarding the five tendencies, either in daily life, or in the context of spiritual practice. Likewise, we should avoid extremist points of view, having a one-sided vision, both on a gross or subtle level. We should always encourage equanimity and benevolence.

The purpose of this book isn't to detail the psychology and behavior of each tendency. It's enough to indicate the framework[5] of the tendencies and the methods one should know and use in order to respond to the difficulties that grasping engenders both in daily life situations and meditation practice.

---

4   In relation to fundamental ignorance, this specific level of ignorance is called "timug" in Tibetan, sometimes translated as "delusion".

5   The framework of the tendencies comprises the fundamental ignorance, the dualistic grasping, the elevation of the tendencies, their recurring aspect, which we can observe, and the state of presence and non-dependent attention which allows their dissolution.

Through its narrow vision, the ego has the habit of wanting to solve problems by isolating them from the many interactions that lead to their emergence.

These conditioned and conditioning tendencies, through which we identify ourselves, come into recurring conflicts with our daily reality. They produce and reinforce multitudes of disturbing emotions.

Disturbing emotions

As long as the veil of ignorance is present and the nature of our mind is not realized, the play of fundamental tendencies, also called "habitual tendencies", will continue, more or less intensely, depending upon the level of grasping.

The dependent ego constantly needs the manifestation of inner and outer phenomena, gross or subtle, in order to perpetuates its existence.

What is called the "conscious part of the ego" in the West is conditioned.

As we said before, it reacts through attraction, if a phenomenon is pleasant and comforting, by repulsion if what arises is unpleasant, or by indifference and ignorance if the response is neither pleasant nor unpleasant. This reaction is conditioned by past experiences. Phenomena themselves don't display labels such as, "good", "bad", etc. Rather our judgments come from our prior conditioning and are projected onto objects of immediate perception.

Conflicts and disturbing emotions

The relationship between conflicts and disturbing emotions must also be clarified.

Conflicts can be explicit in the sense that what is present in the moment is directly experienced as being unpleasant or painful; physically, emotionally, or morally.

Explicit conflicts are always linked to the duality between what is happening and our conditioning. Conflicts also exist implicitly within us in the form of traces and predispositions (vasanas[6]). Deprivations in the past turn into desires, which translate into projections and expectations. This conditioning, which we are not aware of, distances us from the present moment.

Our conditioned reactions to the arising of sensations or images that we consider painful or aggressive is another characteristic of our recurring conflictual functioning within the three spheres. Because we do not experience sensations or images directly, our reactions further reinforce the traces and predisposition.

Our lack of direct experience also elicits already known emotionally conditioned responses.

The three spheres of self, other and their division are conditioned and interdependent. They exist in relationship to each other. Together, these spheres form a determinate ensemble, a unity called the "psychic continuum". For the ego, this type of knitting between and within the spheres ensures duration, and solidity. This continuum is thus closely linked to the way we grasp time and continuity. We think that time has an existence as such.

The psychic continuum solidifies our vision of the past, and projects a future. We anticipate that what

---

6   Vasana: imprint, trace or karmic impregnation.

has been, will continue, both the positive and the negative. For as long as it is seen as a unity, we think our existence in its duration is immutable. Change is consequently slow and difficult.

Our conditioned past masks the present moment, which is always new. The present moment is our only chance to experience something we have never experienced before. The present moment is the only time in our life when awareness is actual. It offers us the only opportunity we have to direct our existence towards a better future. Our habit of holding onto the past and projecting a future hide this precious moment where everything is possible.

Loosing this precious opportunity, which is maintained by the illusion of the ego is a disaster. It is epitomized in the traditional saying that we "Come back from the land of jewels with empty hands".

We think that we are sixty years old. This is an aberration. How can we own the past or the future? Does the past still exist? What future already exists?

Thinking we are sixty years old is merely exercising an abusive right of ownership! Still, we feel we can own a past, which no longer exits. Why are we at all surprised that we keep suffering from past disturbing circumstances?

In the same way, we pretend to already own the future. Why are we surprised that we become anxious about a hypothetical future that has not yet become?

We project duration that doesn't exist, onto everything that appears in the moment. The present moment is hidden by our idea of time, of things and ourselves. We constantly project a hypothetical future, an existence that has no reality. We play with our present in the same way a gambler does in the Sleight-of-Hand game, called "Bonneteau"[7] in French. Gamblers are convinced they know which cup conceals the playing card, but most of the time they are wrong. May we never become sellers of false recipes.

In order to practice the six Buddhist virtues leading to enlightenment— patience, discipline, generosity, courage, concentration, and wisdom— even at a very basic level, we need a great deal of kindness. Challenges and experience teach us humility.

Disturbing emotions are manifold. The Buddha is said to have given eighty-four thousand teachings to resolve the eighty-four thousand kinds of disturbing emotions. All emotions are based on the five energetic tendencies mentioned earlier.

With the experience of presence that is acquired through meditation practice, we can observe the energetic tendency at the base of emotions as they arise during the day. For example, each instance of anger or desire, even the smallest, is an opportunity to connect with its origin, a particular energetic tendency.

Once we have become skilled at seeing the essence of phenomena, we can experience the essential wisdom within our emotions and energetic tendencies.

For most of us, awareness of the essence of phenomena grows very gradually. But each step on the path leads us to feeling better throughout our life.

---

7   The game of "Bonneteau" (Sleight-of-Hand) is a money game in which a gambler tries to keep track of a hidden card as a "bonneteur" swaps three cards under cups.

Our ego's centered nature, which is controlled by desire and aversion, can easily lead us to exaggerate the benefits of meditation. However, the power of duality is such that we must recognize that progress only happens one small step at a time.

In what follows, we will present the meditation practices that allow us to enter the simplicity of the moment, in the benevolent expression of being. These practices are both for practitioners and people who do not yet practice but would like to.

Those who are already practicing an authentic spiritual path will appreciate this song of the Dharma[8] which will gladden their hearts.

---

8 Dharma : Sanskrit term meaning "teaching" in general, and "Buddhist teaching" in particular. The Dharma is one of Buddhism's three jewels.
The three jewels are the Buddha (the Awakened One), the Dharma (the Teaching) and the Sangha (the Community).

Illusion of free will and dependent attention

Free will is usually interpreted as a person's ability to choose and make decisions. In order to assess our freedom, let's observe our attention. What follows are guidelines that shouldn't be read as suggestions or opinions with which one should agree in an abstract way. Rather these guidelines describe an essential and vital practice that can be accomplished and validated through observation and experimentation.

It is sufficient to observe our experience for twenty-four hours to realize that our attention is usually absorbed by what is happening. To become certain of this, we just need to observe ourselves over time. Because the ego believes it is free, it doesn't appreciate how it is totally caught up in its totally conditioned behavior. Observing our limits over the course of a lifetime can significantly reduce our pride tendency. Realizing that we have limited capacity in the development of a non-dependent attention makes us humbler and less pretentious.

Through specific and attentive observation, we discover how our own and other people's attention unfolds over time, in everyday life. We then notice several different characteristics.

Very often, our attention depends upon what is happening in our field of perception. Whether visually or through the other senses of perception, as soon a sensation arises, our attention is drawn to it. The stronger, the more shocking, the more surprising what appears, the more immediate the movement of our attention.

Our attention can become so totally consumed by fear, surprise, and other reactions that everything that surrounds the object of our dependent attention is barely perceived or doesn't even register at all. The greater the intensity of what is happening, the less we are aware of ourselves. We could say that phenomena exist within us, while for us, our own awareness of being is absent.

At other times, phenomena arise in our inner space: feelings, sensations, emotions, and thoughts. The more intense, surprising, negative, or painful the phenomenon is, the more exclusively our attention turns towards it. All the rest of our self disappears, to the extent that sometimes we are no longer aware of our body or the outside world.

We therefore only have a partial and sequential awareness of the world and of ourselves. Moreover, our attention is dependent upon what is happening, upon what arises outside or within us. Our awareness of the world and of ourselves is not only sequential, it is also limited to one object of attention at a time.

This focus of our attention therefore withdraws us from the world and from ourselves.

The conscious and awareness

When we perceive what's around and within us, the external or internal context to our sense of self, our attention grasps an object in one or the other of these inner or outer spaces.

Most of the time, what our attention lands on is not consciously chosen. It is also sequential: the duration of our conditioned attention depends upon how an external or internal object of perception imposes itself.

The terms "conscious" and "awareness" can have several meanings. For example, we can talk about, "Being conscious of someone's problem", "political awareness", etc. The meaning of the words conscious and awareness in these examples is different from what we are talking about when referring to awareness.

In the Buddhist context, awareness is a field. Because of our state of ignorance, this field is veiled and unrecognized. We grasp phenomena manifesting in this field as existing in an absolute way, within themselves, and uncompounded.

Veil of dualistic grasping

From this mistaken perception, we experience our sense of self through phenomena. Our sense of self depends on them. Phenomena are a mirror in which our sense of self is grasped as a "me". That is experienced as an entity existing from its own side, intrinsically and not compounded.

From these two, self and other, a third is born, division. Again, division is experienced as real, and absolute and it generates suffering. Division is like a wound that never heals. Each new division in our life, no matter how small, reopens the wound. Everything we do is intended to be a healing balm, a way to fill the gap, reducing our suffering and help us escape the isolation of loneliness.

Dualistic grasping permeates every perception. It pervades our experience of all external phenomena, as well as everything we sense and feel within ourselves.

Any object of perception can reactivate an imprint related to the primordial separation. Our wounds and everything that we consider negative is denied, refused, and repressed. This is precisely what strengthens imprints. This reinforces and feeds the division between the conscious and so-called unconscious aspects[9] of our mind.

The conscious component is a small fraction of the whole. It is like a narrow field. It is a sliver within the vast spacelike field of pure awareness.

We almost always identify ourselves with mental phenomena, with rational thinking, what we call consciousness, whereas these are only phenomena happening in the limited field of the conscious.

Rational thinking is organized thinking that is defined by causes, consequences, and results. It has

---

9   While the term unconscious has more currency, in the West, in this context sub-conscious is more appropriate.
In a Buddhist context, the semantic weakness of the term unconscious resides in carrying the sense that it has an independent existence, whereas subconscious is a less solidifying term.
The term unconscious also implies that something impermanent exists as such. Subconscious on the other hand is a less solidifying term.

a logical sequence that responds to what we learned in classical education.

Its functioning at the conscious level is coherent and reasonable. It comes from conscious mental activity, i.e. the reality with which individuals identify when they say "I think therefore I am". Which means that we believe we are that which thinks, that which thinks in a way that is organized through our education.

Rational thinking are thoughts with which we identify. It contrasts with a mental activity in which we do not grasp or conceptualize_what we perceive—a mental activity with which we are not identify ourselves, not reducing ourselves to our thoughts.

We distinguish rational thought from what is managed by emotions, and by the unconscious dynamics that are generally neither visible nor perceived. These unconscious dynamics are what manifests in dreams. Their logic is distinct from the logic of rational thinking. The logic of dreams is strongly influenced by disturbing emotions.

We experience the content of our dreams differently than our conscious activity. In dreams, rational thinking manifests itself as anything that appears above the earth or above the water. Rational thought distinguishes trees as a birch, an oak, or a poplar, etc. While the deeper, unconscious activity, simply sees a tree.

We don't recognize how restricted the conscious field is since this is all that we are aware of. Let's take an example, if spacelike awareness is represented as a large, dark room, the conscious would be like the beam of light from a torch. We identify with the objects that are illumined by the beam of light, the mental phenomena. We focus our attention on the illuminated objects. We get totally absorbed. We don't notice the light.

When spacelike awareness is fully realized, it is called "nature of mind", or the "awakened state". When it is veiled, or obscured, as is the case for us, it is called the "Alaya-Vijnana", or "storehouse-consciousness".

If we are attentive, we can see how the veiled state works. When we are awake, we identify with a self. Similarly, in a nightmare, our ego is still at play, for example, it identifies with "the one" who is being chased by a monster. We don't realize that there is no reality to this.

This shows us that the ego, which seeks to preserve its integrity, functions even while we are sleeping.

When we wake up, what do we say? "Last night, I dreamed that a monster was chasing me! What does this mean?"

Our aim is to become aware of our dreams, not to interpret them. We should firstly notice that, as the dreamer, we identify ourselves with the one who is pursued, even though while we are dreaming there is only one mind. The same one mind produces the person who is pursued, the monster, the chase, the setting in which the attempt to escape takes place, as well as the other various objects and characters participating in the drama.

As the dreamer, we don't realize that this dream reveals our divided mind. This dream reveals: the self or ego we identify with; what we don't want in our life (any threat to our existence, the monster); our attempts to escape it when it is our own mind;

and the pursuit in the dream, which reveals both our rejection of and need for reunification.

Through this type of dream, we should become aware that division and suffering can continue and worsen throughout our life, without us ever reflecting on this. To realize this, it is essential to observe our own mind.

Through observation, we can notice the division we make between self and other, and between an inside and an outside space.

The division happens within the perception of all gross and subtle phenomena, both exterior and interior.

Therefore, we should apply ourselves in not grasping an inside or an outside space and focus instead on the field of our attention that surpasses these limits.

While training ourselves in this type of observation, we keep all our sensory doors open. Awareness includes taste, olfactory, auditory, visual, and mental objects of perception. Regarding mental objects of perception (thoughts), we realize that, while we perceive these in our meditation, awareness itself is beyond[10] these thoughts. Awareness cannot be reduced to mental phenomena.

Our training lets us see how the ego uses all six sensory appearances as a mirror to confirm its own

---

10 As explained in the "Ocean of Certainty" (*) [Oral transmission received by the author over 40 years], we can use the term "beyond" at this point in the explanation even though, ultimately, it is inadequate. Indeed, there are no thoughts outside the mind and there is no mind beyond thoughts.
(*)The "Ocean of Certainty" is a book written by the 9th Karmapa (1556-1603), the head of the Kagyu School of Tibetan Buddhism. The book includes teachings on Shiné, Laktong, and Mahamudra.
See "Ocean of Certainty", Ninth Karmapa, Wangchuk Dorjes, Commentary by Traleg Kyabgon, KTD Publications, 2011, Woodstock, NY, United States.

existence. Therefore, it is essential to progress in the meditation practice of non-grasping.

It takes time for this part of our training to become integrated. Then the real training in meditation can begin.

As we saw earlier, meditation is about realizing that our attention is dependent on what arises outside. Then our meditation is motivated by seeking freedom in non-dependence. Arrogant practitioners who believe that they have already mastered meditation are like addicts who claim they can end their addiction whenever they want.

Once we are aware that our attention is controlled by objects of perception, we can begin our meditation practice using a small external object to support our attention, this is called using a "formal support". Or we can use an "informal support of attention", such as our breathing.

We place our attention on the support, without cultivating any idea, without judgment, and without creating any internal commentary about it. We simply perceive, remaining in the perception.

It is customary to practice in a traditional posture. There are several variants according to different schools of meditation. The posture instructions are transmitted to the practitioner by the meditation master. Be cautious of the numerous and experienced sellers of illusions who mislead beginners: looseness in the posture and laxity in the mind can only lead to confusion and giving up.

We call "fixing the unfixed mind" the capacity to stabilize the attention on any support, even for a short time, and to notice distractions before invariably returning to the support, without any judgment.

The duration of our stable attention is extended by always enhancing clarity.

Then the practitioner remains attentive to a chosen support. When mental phenomena appear, they are not linked to an activity of the conscious (thoughts) but emerge from the unconscious field.

Through training, practitioners who use a support of attention are able to stay connected to their consciously chosen support, without being distracted, while being aware of the emergence of phenomena. At this stage, attention that was previously dependent, moved around by objects of perception, becomes non-dependent. Practitioners then need to establish non-dependent attention over time, which means awareness from moment to moment.

I previously mentioned "cognitive grasping". Cognitive grasping is the grasping of an object of perception by a subject who perceives it and thinks of it as distinct. The sense of separation or division between the perceiver and the object of perception from a state of ignorance.

These three, self, other and division—are called "the three spheres". In a process or reification, they are grasped as three distinct things: (1) the distinctive mode—which are initially conceived, (2) the conceptual grasping—as solid and durable units, and (3) the materialized grasping.

Unconscious negative tendencies arise from this reification. When the arbitrary interplay of the three spheres ceases, then the natural functioning of the mind is based on the wisdoms and flows from unity.

Duality affects everyone, and as such, the five unconscious negative tendencies are all active in each of us.

The unconscious negative tendency that dominates us determines our primary behavioral responses. The other four tendencies operate in a supportive manner. Our dominant energetic tendency is recurrent and manifests whenever a conflict occurs. At times however another tendency may take over.

Our dominant tendency, as well as the other four tendencies, are present in all our activities. This includes sleep activities—the postures and movements of our body when we are asleep—as well as the dynamic content manifested in our dreams.

The energetic tendencies are also present in our daily life. They manifest in the rhythm and characteristics of our mental activity, in the orientation of our particular interests, in the way we relate to our circumstances and challenges. The tendencies impact our psychology, our bodily and mental postures, our behavior, where we live, the structure of our relationships and what matters in our lives.

We might believe there is an element of luck or chance at play in our life, when in fact our unconscious dynamics are at work leading us, often repeatedly, towards particular circumstances and certain people.

Among the different behavioral families, the materializing dynamic of the ego is found in the negative aspect of Ratna, pride. People in whom the Ratna tendency dominates need to experience the durability, the solidity, and the permanence of the ego. They believe this can be found by grasping objects, material goods, a social position, which they believe to be solid proof of their own existence.

They experience an irrepressible need for power

and possessions: a need to constantly expand their territory, their sphere of influence into all areas of their life. This is a symptom of their fear of finitude, disappearance, loss of power, influence, possessions, honor, etc.

In the negative aspect of the tendencies, the clinging to material forms paves the way for intense future suffering for people who are predominantly dominated by the negative aspect of the Ratna tendency. At some point, people with this tendency will have to renounce everything they are attached to, all the hallmarks of power, their physical health, everything that affirms their existence. Each stage of their decline will appear like a new death.

As such, people with a Ratna tendency must train to reduce their attachment and grasping to material forms.

Attention to the body

From among the different means that support progress, "attention to the body" is an excellent practice. The practice of attention to the body is based on discursive meditation with the notion of time. We practice this form of meditation until achieving some results.

Usually, the body is the basis of our identification. We define our self from our body, from our appearance, and from what is inside our bodily envelope.

When we practice attention to the body, we develop the intention to pay attention to our global tactile sensation. We train ourselves in perceiving the sensation we have of our bodily envelope in its immediacy. The tactile sensation becomes the point of reference from which we perceive the space within and the space outside our bodily envelope. We try to have an accurate representation of our bodily envelope, as if we were looking at our body from outside.

The practice of attention to the body involves attending to the insubstantial body, through a tactile sensation. It has the virtue of bringing attention back to the fixed point of the sensation of the body, of the feeling of being attached to it, and to the idea of a sense of self, instead of letting oneself be carried away by phenomena.

We thus become aware of the posture of our body, and aware of the sensations we experience inside it, in their immediacy, while simultaneously being aware of what is happening around us. We train to do this more and more precisely.

We begin by repeatedly observing whether past time exists. After many observations, we answer "yes" or "no". Then, we repeatedly observe if the future already exists, and similarly respond with "yes" or "no".

If our answer is "no, these do not exist", how can we possibly explain our usual and strong certainty about being thirty, forty or sixty years old? The projection of our duration is very powerful because it is unconscious.

Isn't past time a completely relative notion, depending on other notions such the present and the future?

Finally, does the present moment exist in itself? Isn't the present moment the future of a past moment and the past of a future moment?

Does the present moment last a second, a tenth, a thousandth, a billionth fraction of a second?

This is what Albert Einstein demonstrated in the theory of relativity. Time is a variable notion depending on the state of consciousness, and on the place from which perception happens in relation to the place where the perceived object is located.

When we are disconnected from the relativity of time, we attribute duration, solidity, and self-existence to all phenomena.

The relativity of time is inseparable from the relativity of all the objects of perception that manifest themselves in time, including our own body.

We keep this notion of relativity in mind and apply it to everything. We need to realize how being in the moment is a magnificent opening to life. Being in the moment dissolves all the negativity that solidify and reify our ego.

By constantly reanimating a negative past that no longer exists, the ego cloths what's alive, the present, in the dullness of our memories. Suffering and the heavy weight of things and circumstances take place over a very long time, making progress difficult.

The relativity of time and what is manifested in it will be emphasized in the practice of attention to the body. Prior to this practice, we must have successfully accomplished the following:

(1) Developed our capacity to bring focused attention for a brief moment to any support.

(2) Extended the duration of our attention.

(3) Maintained our link with the support. This lets us be aware of phenomena as they emerge from the unconscious.

These three steps need to be accomplished prior to entering the practice of attention to the body.

During the day, we constantly experience tactile sensations, but we are rarely aware of them. Our perceptions depend on circumstances. We don't choose to experience these sensations, they happen. They are partial, and most of the time, only involve a small area on the surface of our body.

Awareness perceives tactile sensations in their immediacy. We don't feel through our past body. It no longer exists. We don't feel through our future body. It doesn't yet exist. Our body isn't solid either. It is only composed of particles of atoms which are themselves subatomic energy. Our body has no intrinsic existence. It isn't unitary.

Through training, a practitioner can acquire a clearer sensation and global representation of their body.

Usually, the representation of our body as well as the sensation of our body, are only momentary (only lasting for short moments) and partial (we are only aware of a fraction of them). The representation and sensation of our body depend upon circumstances.

We therefore practice associating the sensation and the representation of the body, in order for these two to become unified and comprehensive, instead of intermittent and partial. We use the association of the sensation and the representation of our body as a permanent guide, an Ariadne's thread[11].

When I talk about the practice of attention to

---

11 Translator's note, the Ariadne's thread is a metaphor originating in Greek mythology in which a thread serves as a guide to help Ariadne retrace her steps to get out of a difficult situation.

the body, I mean associating the sensation and the representation of our body. This association constitutes a reliable reference that connects us to the state of instantaneous, unobstructed, and unveiled space-like awareness.

Like an Ariadne's thread it guides us in functioning independently of circumstances. We make this Ariadne like thread the support of our attention and intention. We intend to relate to the global tactile sensation. And we remain aware of this global tactile sensation. This association is called, "attention to the Self (an individual sense of self without any grasping at an independent existence) and to the meaning". It means that the support of our attention is a source of the revelation of the mind perceiving itself. The mind reveals itself, unveiled, as it is!

Thus, what happens within or outside us no longer obscures the mind's capacity for seeing through what is called, "higher vision" (Laktong[12] in Tibetan). The absence of grasping when linked to a stable capacity for tactile attention naturally transmutes the negative play of the tendencies, thoughts, and emotions, into their positive aspects.

The practice of attention to the body helps us develop the function of the mind which allows to perceive even when the eyes are closed. I this case, our perception directly originates from the field of space.

Of course, prior to realizing the qualities that allow the higher vision, we must cultivate the many methods of concentration.

---

12 Laktong, or "lhaktong" in Tibetan, vipashana in Sanskrit means higher vision. It is the capacity of the mind that arises from the state of concentration. This capacity allows one to know the nature of phenomena and the nature of the mind, as it is, i.e. emptiness.

In order to stay motivated, practitioners should be aware of their state of dependence, and of the suffering created by their conditioning, and by impermanence and death. Being aware of this will support the development of patience, discipline, generosity, courage, concentration and finally wisdom. This is the path that the Buddha recommends.

When practitioners reach the higher vision they no longer perceive emotional phenomena as defects. Phenomena allow us to become aware of awareness, the consciousness that produces and perceives phenomena. Awareness is featureless, and unaffected. Awareness is, fundamentally, who we are.

The awareness that both produces and perceives phenomena doesn't shut down when phenomena cease. For example, when we are asleep, awareness doesn't disappear. It remains even when we are unaware of it. It always remains in its potential qualities.

The tactile sensation is like a knot in a handkerchief, it reminds us of awareness itself, which is beyond the perception of a self, an other and a division. This is called "beyond the three spheres", beyond the notions of subject, object, and division.

The practice of attention to the body is not just a remedy for the Ratna tendency. Before being transmuted, all five energetic tendencies should be observed. It takes time, but any motivated practitioner can progress.

Time for the ego and time for meditation

Within the dualistic state, we continually project an illusory concept of time. In fact, the past no longer exists, and the future doesn't exist either. Therefore, no duration exists as such.

The faculty of awareness for pure perception is instantaneous. However, our capacity for instantaneous perception is veiled. So much so that the conscious, associated with constructed thought, grasps at phenomena thinking they have a duration.

Does the present moment have an existence of its own? Does a moment last for a second, a tenth, a hundredth, a ten thousandth of a second? Can a fraction of the present moment exist in itself? If it was the case, this fraction would still have a beginning and an end, it would be divisible. So, there is no present moment in and of itself.

If time is relative, gross or subtle phenomena that have characteristics whether interior or exterior are also relative. All phenomena, as well as time, are divisible into parts, atoms, and subatomic particles, etc. There are no partless particles, only dimensionless points of virtuality. Isn't this virtuality the mind before the appearance of any formal thought?

Our way of perceiving the duration of time, consists of attributing a duration and a reality to phenomena which are perceived in time, which is relative. We can compare this with our way of seeing movies.

Time and emotions

When we watch a movie, we see a unity, a continuity of actions over time. Our ego mind doesn't perceive each of the images individually. We do not see twenty-four discrete images per second. What provokes our emotions is the fact that we hold onto the idea of duration and the phenomena within it. If we weren't seeing and projecting a unity; if we were perceiving each image independently from its context, we would not feel the same emotion.

We can recall how in earlier years, when a film broke during a screening, people would immediately express their disappointment.

The ego-mind, which arises through the six senses of perception[13], doesn't like to see its own projection disintegrate.

---

13 Six senses of perception: in Buddhism, we identify five sensory faculties and one extrasensory faculty.

The taste, smell, hearing, sight, and touch faculties express themselves through the sense organs.

The extrasensory faculty comes from the knowing faculty of the mind. Mental phenomena do not perceive themselves. It's awareness that perceives mental phenomena. We have the capacity to perceive without using the senses of perception.

When we are in the immediacy of the moment, we don't perceive things as we usually do. The world of coarse sense perceptions, which is usually perceived as existing in time, doesn't present itself with the same density, with the same appearance of reality[14]. Nothing can be grasped, and nothing can trigger disturbing emotions. These only exist for the ego-mind that's enslaved by time and coarse appearances.

Time, space, and phenomena only exist relatively to our state of consciousness. We are conditioned to only grasp what is coarse. We take in the appearance of phenomena through a solidified notion of time. We ignore their relativity. Likewise, from a fundamental point of view, we do not know who we really are,

The way we solidify everything makes us suffer. Being in the immediacy of the moment lets us relativize everything. Once the veils that obscures perceptions vanish, the all-knowing qualities of what is called "the nature of mind" open up new perspectives allowing us be more in touch with what is truly alive.

The process of unveiling the nature of mind, by severing our ignorance doesn't reduce our capacity to see the phenomenal world in its relative nature. There is no denial or devaluation of the phenomenal world. Rather this realization puts things back in order. This new order becomes a source of great benefits.

---

14 The appearance of reality is similar, for example, to the state we are in when we wake up from a disturbing dream that seemed real, yet all that remains are only some memory fragments of it.

Psychic continuum,
source of paralysis and incapacity

The ego lives in dependence on phenomena. It exists through grasping at them. It needs to see and feel that phenomena are solid and durable. As well as a relentless compulsion to be involved with phenomena, the ego is caught up in the powerful dynamic of attachment. The awareness that exists beyond the ego-mind sees phenomena in their immediacy whereas the dynamic of attachment subjugates phenomena to what is known and conditioned.

Our conditioning is determined by our life experiences and our education, especially those events that have strongly marked and disturbed us.

We immediately associate name and form with what we perceive in the moment, as a function of what we have learned through our education and past emotional experiences. When we perceive something, most of what we experience is related to the past. The momentariness of the contact with the perceived object is occluded by our notion of time, which doesn't itself exist. The present instant is covered by past emotions and feelings of solidity and durability. These feelings give us a reassuring, but illusory, impression that we exist, no matter how disturbing these past contents were.

The way we perceive objects of perception triggers a resurgence of past impressions, which enslaves the present to the past.

And so it goes, one moment to the next. This is called the "continuum". The continuum gives the ego the impression that it is lasting and solid which is reassuring. In the meantime, this confines the continuum. It massively limits our possibilities for progress and change.

Therefore, seeing the world through this psychic continuum produces huge feelings of inadequacy and paralysis.

The play of negative tendencies, also called "habitual tendencies", unconsciously express themselves through this continuum. As a result, throughout our lives, our negative tendencies invariably lead us to encounter and replay the same kind of situations to which we respond to in the same conditioned ways.

This flood of mental phenomena, memories, and projections, looks similar to what we experience when we watch a movie. Past experiences, images, are associated with projections about a future that doesn't exist, and likewise with the past. The only image, the only object that exists in the moment isn't even perceived.

The concept of time is relative. At the conscious level, we are subject to the notions of time and space. At this level, the gross level, we have the impression that we need time to change. For example, to acquire tranquility when we are restless, or want to acquire a profession that we do not yet know, we need time.

But from another point of view, when we are able to put our attention on a mental phenomenon, in the moment we do it, this mental phenomenon dissolves. The ego envisions everything in time. But the meditator can experience the relativity of time. Similarly, at the dream level, we can transcend the notions of dream and space. We see reality directly, independently of concepts.

A meditative experience of samadhi is an immediate emergence. Unconsciously, it may have matured for years. But when our natural state of mind reveals itself, the experience is lightning.

We then enter the direct nature of mind instead of the time of ego and duality. The meditative state is beyond human time, notions of duration, or experience. In one samadhi moment, flows of causal sequences can appear and be purified.

Now, let's consider the six transcendent virtues or perfections, which include generosity, discipline, and patience. How can we assess someone's patience, for example? If we only rely on an instantaneous picture, what can we see of anyone's patience? Nothing really. In such instance, to really perceive someone's virtues, we need time. And yet, if someone is patient over time, they are also patient, in the moment, moment by moment.

Grasping and duality

If dualistic grasping provokes these negative sequences, its cessation should suppress them or, more exactly, "not produce them".

This an important distinction because the word "suppress" contains the sense of opposition, of rejection. The idea implies that obstacles could have an intrinsic and objective reality. However, as we saw earlier, obstacles, like everything else that has characteristics are compounded, and therefore do not have any absolute reality. Besides, what makes a situation durable, what reifies it is our attempt to push it away. Everything we try to stop from happening is perpetuated, or even develops further because we assume it is real.

Since grasping is the cause for being trapped in this continuum, understanding the dynamic of this process should help it dissolve through the cessation of grasping.

Intellectual understanding is useful of course but is only of limited help. For the continuum to stop, we must enter a stabilized realization of non-grasping.

This is difficult. Because the ego thinks it knows what is needed. It stops with a simple intellectual understanding. The ego believes that there is sufficient power in intellectual understanding to produce change, but this is totally wrong. Seeing and intellectual understanding do let us move on towards direct experience. But like knowing and understanding, conceiving, and realizing also need to be distinguished.

Realization is the state of immediate awareness experienced in the moment. We shouldn't put realization in an opposite domain to the mental. With data from the gross senses, the conceptual mind helps us negotiate our way in the gross phenomenal world, as it appears in time.

The mental activity that processes relative phenomena should be considered a defect. The defect consists of thinking that mental activity is awareness itself. Reducing awareness to mental phenomena is an aberration. Being attached to this mistake we make the intellect into an absolute. This is what is called "ignorance".

Only a few minutes of meditation practice is needed to see that when mental phenomena arise, we can be aware of them in the moment they arise. We can be aware of them when they arise because awareness is "beyond" the perceived phenomena.

Direct experience demonstrates that awareness pre-exists phenomena, and that the latter depends on awareness, not the opposite.

Grasping the result as the cause is equivalent to thinking that waves create the ocean. Meditation restores the right order to things; it reveals the natural hierarchy.

Through meditation we recover the right relationship between awareness and the phenomena it produces and perceives.

Through meditation we stop conflating awareness with phenomena. We stop believing that we only exist through phenomena, that our existence depends upon them, which is the fundamental cause of all forms of dependence.

What do we mean by "grasping"? It consists of clinging with absolute certainty to the idea we have of things. Too often it involves taking the ideas about things as being the things themselves.

This happens whenever we think that we've intellectually understood something, and then believe this is knowledge.

This is more damaging when we believe that knowledge is sufficient to change our behavior, and free ourselves from emotions.

Grasping also happens when we believe that by naming an object, let's say a wall as "a wall", that through naming we are identifying the reality of what we perceive.

In fact, we only see a painted surface that covers the plasterboard composed of other layers, glue, breeze block, cement, plaster, etc. What are we grasping then? We are grasping at mere appearances. What are we naming? We are naming mere appearances. Through our six senses of perception, gustatory, olfactory, auditory, visual, tactile, and mental, we only perceive appearances; appearances of thoughts;

appearances of objects; appearances of people; appearances of all the objects of perception.

The six objects of perception are perceived by the six senses. When consciousness perceives these objects, it immediately triggers the processes of duration, and the resurgence of compressed content and projections create an impression of density and reality. This is reinforced by emotional imprints. None of this reflects reality as it is.

There is nothing in phenomena that can give us a feeling of being real: we cannot "really" experience our own existence through dependence on phenomena, nor can we experience it independently of them. Nothing can fill this void, this gap. When we rely upon phenomena to confirm our existence, we actually perceive the world in absentia[15] (i.e. without perceiving it, and without being present. We perceive our memories and projections, but not what is in the moment), things and others give us the right to exist, but it's a fake sense of existence.

We identify with an ego by grasping our body, our emotions, our thoughts, like the wall in the example above.

We call "me" something we haven't experienced. Over time, by focusing exclusively on appearances, we only observe a totally conditioned type of mental functioning. We fail to recognize the pure awareness, which is its base.

When we say, "me", we define ourselves through the envelope of our body, we locate ourselves "inside" it is as if this is who we are. We therefore judge ourselves in relationship to our appearance, the envelop.

---

15   In absentia means in the absence of the person who should be involved.

We can extend this observation and realize that all olfactory, gustatory, auditory, visual, tactile, and mental objects we perceive and name, are unconsciously serving the same purpose: They preserve the illusion of a self which is arbitrarily defined in relationship to a surface, an appearance. The name we associate with this appearance defines a concept. The process of applying names to forms allows us to maintain an illusion that things really exist in and of themselves.

The same process applies to the coarse as well as the subtle, and to outer and inner objects of perception perceived by the six modes of perception.

The spiritual meaning in our existence

The path we follow in our life depends on our intention. This intention is therefore important. The *Ocean of Certainty* states the highest intention as follows, "Through listening and reflection, may I achieve enlightenment and thereby establish all the beings who were my mothers in enlightenment as well".

This intention is called Bodhicitta[16] which is what we develop through our practice. Enlightenment is inseparable from altruism, just as butter is inseparable from milk.

If our intention is self-centered, then everything we do is a mundane activity. If our intention is directed towards others, this is called "Dharma".

---

16 Bodhicitta is the mind oriented towards enlightenment for the benefit of all sentient beings. The relative aspect of this awakening mind is conceptual. What dominates in this idea is to accomplish the benefit of others rather than acting from selfish needs. The ultimate or absolute Bodhicitta is the establishment of the practitioner in a non-conceptual wisdom-mind, the source of universal love.

The fulfillment of Dharma consists of achieving a non-conceptual state, which is the source of all benefits, in order to fulfil our goal of benefiting others. This requires the cessation of the grasping of the three spheres, the grasping of a me, an other and a division between these two.

EGO GRASPING

We must also be aware that we grasp at all appearances, gross or subtle, exterior or interior, to our sense of self, and in doing so we create a division, which is the source of suffering.

In the moment that we attribute an absolute reality to things, we also try to possess those that are pleasant and comforting. People, social positions, material goods, etc. become objects of desire and attachment.

Similarly, we grasp things as real and constantly reject everything that is painful and doesn't comfort us. But by rejecting them, we keep encountering them, since everything that we reject is maintained or even further developed.

While we give attention to what is pleasant and unpleasant, there are also a multitude of phenomena that are neither pleasant nor unpleasant, and which only produce ignorance and disinterest.

When we are able to notice our reactions to phenomena, we can see that in each moment our attraction, repulsion or indifference is conditioned by our past experiences.

Nothing in the instant of its appearing qualifies itself as "good", "bad" or "uninteresting". Especially given that in the moment a phenomenon appears, it is totally new, it has never been experienced before.

THE AWAKENING MINDSET

Developing the awakening mindset, the altruistic mindset supposes that we understand this instantaneous experience which emancipates itself from conditioning. Many times, in our life, we have undoubtedly been an object of repulsion or indifference from others, while longing for attention, interest or kindness. So why do we feed everything that happens through the mill of our conditioning?

Judging people and things through old ideas coming from the past, should seem unfair to us, especially when connecting with a fresh and wholesome mindset brings us happiness. May we see things for what they are without reducing them and ourselves at the same time to a past that no longer exists.

REMINDING OURSELVES OF THE ULTIMATE MEANING

Our intention to move towards an altruistic mindset needs to be frequently recalled—this includes a reminder of the Self, accompanied by the reminder of the ultimate meaning. We return to our intention by tuning into the present moment. In order to do this, it is essential that we find means of recollection.

SUFFERING, DUALITY AND ALTRUISTIC INTENTION

The ego has always held onto a distinction between the sacred and the profane, between good and evil. In the Buddhist context, dualistic grasping and ignorance, are the roots of the ego which produce negative consequences and suffering.

The grasping of the idea of the sacred has its origins and is sustained by the grasping at its opposite, the idea of the profane, or ordinary. Depending upon the partiality of our ego, we are inclined to grasp or reject either the profane or the sacred or vice versa. Consequently, we maintain and develop what we reject.

Because we define ourselves through objects, when we adhere to the pure, we reject the impure and vice versa; we battle against what we reject and make it our greatest enemy. Ultimately, we create conflicts in order to confirm that we exist.

The same process occurs for all objects of perception: people, circumstances, conditions, etc. When for example we talk about starting a diet, or commencing a practice, we think that there is a unitary self-engaging in these actions, but, in fact, there is no unity.

Our ego is composed of contradictory currents which manifest in the present moment. One part of us says, "I am starting a diet" while the other part says to itself "it's ok to eat another mouthful, and another one."

One current within us begins a practice, and another then abandons it. However, we think of both currents as the same "me", whereas nothing like this exists fundamentally: like all phenomena, the self is composed.

Observation convinces us that a game of alternation is constantly at play in all domains: pure and impure, East and West, masculine and feminine, reason and feeling, right and left, etc.

We diminish the meaning of our existence when we attribute an absolute reality to phenomena which they do not have. This is how we confuse our existence with the events that happen within it, and this is how we confuse awareness with what manifests in it. And the same happens with space: we only give importance to objects, ignoring the fact that without space nothing could exist.

Alternatively, we could consider what assembles and unifies. Our intention towards unity and altruism must be woven with all the moments and circumstances of our existence. It is our intention that gives an elevated meaning to all objects of perception.

PHENOMENA ARE COMPOUNDED

To enter into a normal relationship with phenomena, it is essential to remember the Buddhist teaching that, "All phenomena are compounded" which is this is first of the four seals of dharma[17]. Nowadays, the current scientific worldview confirms this.

Our observation of phenomena helps us recognize that they are all compounded, not unities, and therefore only relatively real. This observation prevents us from attributing any absolute existence to that which is compounded and relative.

NATURE OF MIND

The awakened mind lets us establish a view that connects to the state called "nature of mind". Initially, we do this conceptually until we ultimately abide in it.

---

17 Translator's note, see "*The Four Seals of Dharma*", Lama Khenpo Karma Ngedön, translated by Jourdie Ross, 2021, Rabsel Publications.

SEEDING

If the methods outlined in this book aren't associated with the reminding of the Self, the present moment, and the ultimate meaning, they can only be regarded as ordinary ego-oriented games. But these methods combined with the aspiration hold the superior intention, realizing the nature of mind.

Making aspirations is an essential part of Buddhist practice and must be considered as such by anyone who wants to progress on the path.

We should not confuse aspirations with good intentions. Good intentions arise from a dominating current in our mind at any given time. As such they will be, more or less quickly displaced by an opposite current.

Also, intentions that are expressed too quickly and openly are not based on deep reflection, observation, and determination. Our observation should be refreshed continually. It should include the understanding of the contradictory currents that prevent choice, and which diminish and paralyze our capacities.

Practitioners must understand that fighting the different currents in our mind is a waste of time and depletes our energy. These currents should contribute to our progress. Wasting energy and repeated inefficiency lead to discouragement, fatigue and giving up.

Aspiration is the seed. Indian Tantrism developed in an agrarian culture in which spring and autumn are the seasons for planting crops. Similarly, in daily life, our aspiration, our intention for a practice or a project is formulated at the beginning and at the end of each day.

Our intention for our practice is essential. The conditions are also important. The conditions are effectively the soil that allows the actualization of the potential fruits.

Confidence is important as well. Confidence includes investing ourselves in everything we do while being present and attentive. We have no doubt about the outcome. So long as we do our best, there can be no regret.

The best conditions for sowing are therefore found at the beginning and end of a day, or as we commence and complete an action. These conditions include a relaxed and confident state, concentration, repetition, duration, and a positive affective state, for example devotion[18].

FOUR REMINDERS

Throughout our journey, the teachings we receive are in themselves reminders of the ultimate meaning. For example, the foundation of our discursive meditations consists of the four contemplations. These are actualized through the events that punctuate our daily life.

These four contemplations are:

(1) Impermanence and death.

(2) The suffering inherent in existing in a body.

(3) Causality, our actions have consequences, and

(4) the preciousness of human existence.

---

18 Devotion, we dedicate ourselves to the ultimate goal and profound meaning, or to what's representing them, for example, the lama and the Three Jewels.

These four contemplations help us renounce expectations for an absolute happiness coming from relative and conditioned phenomena. Meditating on the extraordinary value of our existence enables us to realize the ultimate benefit that includes all sentient beings.

Opportunities for reminding and actualisation

We must consider the aspiration and its persistence[19]. When we engage in a practice of deep relaxation or in sitting meditation, the central meaning of our aspiration should be actualized. However, when we formulate our aspiration, are we really present? And when we are present to our aspiration, are we also present to the awareness that perceives it without grasping any self? Are we doing so in time or in the immediacy of the moment?

To meet the optimum conditions in our meditation, we need to train ourselves in one of the forms of attention to tactile sensation or practice of attention to the body (See, *Attention to the body*, page 45). As practitioners we know that time is relative, that the past no longer exists, and the future doesn't yet exist. Therefore, when the tactile sensation becomes the thread of our attention, it means that we are in the present moment.

We repeatedly sow our aspiration in a concentrated state and over time. We develop an aspiration to

---

19 The persistence of aspirations: in the same way that in seated meditation the practitioner formulates wishes towards awakening, when we fall asleep, it is possible to formulate the aspiration to wake up on the phases of dreams, which is the first step towards possibility of becoming lucid in the dream., In the awareness of a distraction or a phenomenon, in the seated practice or in the awakening stage of sleep, the practitioner should see the result of his aspirations and acknowledges these as good signs.

recall. In order to do this, we can anchor specific circumstances and precise actions that we perform frequently, such as opening a door, and we use this as an opportunity to remind ourselves of our aspiration. We remain aware of our sense of self in its immediacy and remember the ultimate meaning that relates to it.

We can do this each time we go through a threshold. Each time we go through a limit, mental or physical; each time we begin or end an action, there is a passage from an interior to an exterior. We can do this for every transition.

Thus, every day, when we wake up and before falling asleep, we develop aspirations towards the ultimate goal. We express our gratitude for still being alive. We frame our day and night by the aspirations, so despite everything that happens, our intention is present.

We dedicate everything to the welfare of all sentient beings, from our most mundane actions, through to the practices we accomplish, and the teachings we hear or give.

Each time we practice asanas[20], pranayamas[21], supine meditation in Shavasana[22], or in a seated posture, we begin with the aspiration towards this goal, and end by dedicating the merits of our practice to the wellbeing of all sentient beings.

We can include our sleep in our practice, but this requires specific conditions. We include dreamless

---

20 Asanas : yoga postures.

21 Pranayamas : mastery of the subtle breath.

22 Shavasana: is a traditional yoga posture in supine position. It is also called the "corpse posture". *See, Deep relaxation, and Shavasana*, page 93.

sleep as well as the so-called "paradoxical" sleep (with dreams). We make an intention to wake up during the dream phases. This is an effective way to get closer to what is deep in our mind. We follow the principle of not trying to interpret the dream. One doesn't engage in this if one is restless or suffering from insomnia.

We dedicate our food to the Buddha, Dharma and Sangha when taking meals, doing it just mentally if the context suggests[23].

We set up a place for our practice, when supporting conditions are still needed. Places of practice, presence of other practitioners, audio and visual media, can also be useful reminders.

We install a place where we can have symbolic offerings representing the goal: candles, incense, bowls and supports of the three jewels. Doing it within a Buddhist framework can be more or less ritualistic. Whatever the case, it is important not to be totally averse to rituals. By observing the routines we already follow before going to bed, when getting up, while eating, etc., we see that everything is actually ritualized. Through this, we can understand that daily rituals can be useful to us.

In any case, the aspiration, the reminder of the Self, and the conditions mentioned above, remain of value in any process of deepening our spiritual practice.

Aside from the practice of attention to the body, which we've already discussed, breathing awareness

---

23 If you are not a Buddhist, take time to consider food as a precious substance, which becomes your flesh and blood, and then becomes your sense of self, the support of your fulfilments.

is another great way to remember. Our breath is not a formal medium. It accompanies us in every moment of our lives. It is therefore a thread for our attention. It is sufficiently constant to constitute a reference point which can help us to not grasp at phenomena.

There are a few different ways to pay attention to our breath. One consists of focusing our attention at the door of the nostrils in the moment-by-moment perception of the flow of the breath.

When practitioners of Vajrayana Buddhism[24] have established a very close connection with their spiritual master, they rely on this connection to reach a conceptless state of presence, called "samadhi"[25]. The Lama then becomes a support that practitioners use to connect to their ultimate goal.

In everyday life, practitioners can also use the Lama as a reminder. Everything that is perceived through their six senses is dedicate to their Lama. They visualize the Lama in various places in their body. When they drink or eat something pleasant, they visualize the Lama in their throat and thus offer what is eaten. They can also visualize the Lama on their shoulder and thus link everything they perceive to their ultimate goal as represented by the Lama.

At bedtime, practitioners visualize the Lama in their heart. Devotion to our spiritual master and, through its intermediacy, to our ultimate goal is a superior means of remembering.

---

24 Vajrayana : the tantric path of Buddhism, sometimes called Mantrayana.

25 Samadhi : establishment in a stable state of absorption and concentration without a concept.

TAKING REFUGE

This is linked to another important moment in the spiritual journey, taking refuge. As Westerners, it might have taken us our whole life to reach conclusions that led us to commit ourselves in a formal way to Buddhism. We do so through the ceremony of taking refuge.

Taking refuge is a special moment in which we give meaning to our existence as a choice coming from our reflection and intimate conviction. Practitioners renew taking refuge every day of their life. As we only exist in the present moment, our intention is made constantly in the moment, and with great fervor.

Our intention, as well as the reminder of the Self we will use, must be extended by a selected practice. This practice can be chosen by the practitioner. However, when practitioners have a strong bond with a spiritual master, they rely on their Lama's opinion and recommendation. Practitioners then report to their Lama and let the teacher guide their progress through precise teachings and practices. Our tailored daily practice, our connection with the Lama who transmitted it to us, and the fact of reporting back to the Lama, are all means of recollection.

TOOLS OF PRACTICE, RETREATS, PILGRIMAGE, MALA AND MANTRAS

• Retreats

Because of their structure, intensive practice retreats are useful. At first, according to practitioners' level of practice and motivation, retreats can be very helpful. We withdraw to a quiet place, somewhere different from our usual place of residence. We then devote ourselves intensively to our practice, without communicating with the outside world. We eat little and stay silent. These rules make it easy to find tranquility and clarity.

Naturally, retreats must be undertaken with the guidance of qualified retreat guide. The above retreat structure is just one example among many types of retreats. These retreats encourage practitioners and are an opportunity to deepen our practices and understanding. They also help us to integrate and stimulate the association of concentration, repetition, and the feeling for, and duration of, the meditative practice and meditative state.

• Pilgrimages

Pilgrimages to sacred places, aspirations, practicing and making offerings are also means of remembering our ultimate intention. Even up to the present day, Tibetan pilgrims continue to make the journey by foot from their home region to pilgrimage places while making prostrations. Every three steps they make a full body length prostration. When they reach their goal, regardless of the distance traveled, they turn around three times and go back the same way.

I have personally participated in and organized such pilgrimages. We travel thousands of kilometers, experiencing the great difficulties and expectations of such journeys, in order to reach the revered places of Buddhism. These journeys leave a very strong imprint on our mind. Meeting masters, practicing in these places, making offerings for people who are suffering or deceased, produce traces that linger in our minds throughout our lives and feed our altruistic mindset.

Meeting with sages who bear excellent qualities and receiving their blessing, reinforces our motivation. The same is true of blessing supports that we carry with us such as blessing cords and Katas[26].

People who don't follow any particular tradition with its specific rituals should still maintain a connection to the deeper meaning of their life.

Just as important as outer pilgrimages is the inner pilgrimage, which is made through the development of love and compassion.

The love we feel during our life for our mother, our father, our close companions, or our children should be used to broaden our human qualities so that they serve all sentient beings. Our loved ones, become the ways and means for connecting us to love and peace. They are places of inner pilgrimage that take us to the extraordinary place that is our loving heart.

• Mala and mantras

Another means for evoking an aspiration is through the use of a mala. For many Westerners the mala reminds them of a rosary. It is used in all regular Tibetan Buddhist practices.

The mala allows us to record the number of mantras or practices we perform. Several kinds of seeds or beads can be used to make a mala. In

---

26 Katas : silk scarfs practitioners offer or receive to honor guests, during a meeting with a spiritual master.

particular, seeds of the Bodhi tree[27] are used. Sometimes an open eye is seen on the seed.

Lotus seeds are also used to make mala beads. Lotus flowers, especially the sacred ones, are magnificent. The lotuses take root in the mud, which represents what is impure. Yet, from the mud, rises this enormous flower which opens its corolla far above the surface of the water. Its immaculate whiteness and total blossom symbolize pure vision and ultimate awakening.

There are many references to the lotus in postural work, for example, the lotus posture "padmasana" or the shanti mudra. One of the most famous mantras[28] of Tibetan Buddhism, "om mani padme hum", is often translated as "the Jewel in the Lotus." A famous teaching by the Buddha is called, *the Lotus Sutra*[29]. The chakra that symbolizes the awakening process is called "Thousand Petals" chakra. Lotus seeds and Bodhi tree seeds are therefore commonly used to symbolize what practitioners sow in their own limited mind while aiming for enlightenment.

The mala is a support for counting the hundreds, the thousands, the hundreds of thousands and finally the millions of mantras recited in practices. During mantra repetitions, practitioners remain focused on the support which opens them to the positive

---

27 The Buddha attained enlightenment under a Bodhi tree, in Bodhgaya, India.

28 Mantra : Thought tool. Through perfect repetition, the mantra protects the practitioner from what arises from grasping at a past that no longer exists and a future that has not yet become. The mantra introduces the practitioner to the present where the inherent wisdom realizes the essence-emptiness of the mantra and the qualities it conveys.

29 Sutras are the Buddhist equivalent of the Bible's verses. The 84,000 teachings of the Buddha are called the "Kangyur" in Tibetan. The Tibetan Buddhist canon also includes the commentaries by scholars and philosophers, called the "Tengyur".

potentialities inherent in the dynamic wisdoms of the mind.

Mantras are spoken aloud, then whispered and finally formulated mentally, which is the deepest way. The recitation can be associated with a visualization.

Practitioners may connect their body, speech, and mind with the mantra and its object. The mala always allows for the participation of the body in the ultimate sense. For example, in order to remember the nature of the mind and stay connected with our pure intention via our body, we keep seeding our mala while we talk.

We have spoken already about the importance of the Refuge Vows. All vows are means of reminding us of the spiritual nature of existence. Amongst Buddhist Vows, the Bodhisattva Vows are unique, since in the Bodhisattva Vows we commit all our actions and practices to the welfare of others.

AWARE AND PRESENT

Without reminders our existence has no spiritual meaning. Being alive, being a "living being", being present, fully present to our "beingness", has nothing to do with the past or the future.

Wisdom resides in the capacity for our present and aware sense of self to reflect on the past and learn from it. If we identify with what no longer exist, our aliveness diminishes. Using the past wisely, and being guided by our intentions, actions and behaviors, support us in achieving a future that will be good for all.

ULTIMATE INTENTION

The strength of negative and conditioned intentions which manifests itself in the present has been fed through time by a succession of many intentions and acts. However, this buildup of negative intentions no longer has any existence, and its strength is only contained in the grasping we make of it in the present moment.

If we are aware and present, we can initiate the sowing of another imprint of intentions based on love and a good heart towards others. We then direct this towards the future experience of all others, wishing that they can be free of all obstacles and delusions.

WHY ARE SLEEPING AND DREAMING SO IMPORTANT?

I previously mentioned the place of sleep and dream in our life, particularly in relationship to time. When we reach the age of sixty, we have spent twenty years of our life asleep. Our lack of interest in this state is somewhat shocking.

How would we react if we were sentenced to twenty years in prison? Or if there were twenty years of train strikes, or twenty years without pay? We would talk about it endlessly!

And yet, is there a more important time than our sleep, an activity more essential than dreaming? Why are our sleep state and dream activity important? We should consider this matter firstly from the state of duality and then from the viewpoint of non-duality.

Let us recall that the mind of an awakened being—a Buddha—is an infinite field of space, whereas the mind of a human being—even someone highly endowed with many qualities is like the space in the eye of a needle.

We can compare this tiny space in the eye of a needle to a vast room plunged into darkness. In this tiny space, the field of our conscious is comparable to the beam of a flashlight that illuminates an object in this vast room.

Normally, we should at least recognize the light beam as being our individual consciousness, which doesn't depend on the illuminated object. "But, no!" Our ego takes itself for the illuminated phenomenon and mistakes it for consciousness.

When an object moves or makes a noise, we should normally avoid reducing our conscious to these movements, or making it depend on them. Logically, the vast space of the large lit room—consciousness—shouldn't be reduced to movements, and our attention shouldn't depend on what happens. "Well, no!" But instead, the ego hangs on like a leech that doesn't want to let go of what it believes is vital to its perpetuation.

Our conscious—the narrow beam of the torch—identifies itself with phenomena instead of being aware that it is actually illuminating them. This mistake weakens us. We depend on circumstances, on what appears under the flashlight instead of simply noticing that phenomena occur.

The ego therefore feels compelled to follow or even worse to seek and desire phenomena. Since the ego depends on phenomena, they falsely feel reassuring. Phenomena are the security blanket of ego-desire-attachment.

Conversely, the ego also feels compelled to defend itself, to avoid and to resist phenomena, in all the forms that they may appear. The ego is constantly on guard! In paranoid delusion stemming from anger-aversion, the ego suspects any appearance that could question its existence. This happens because we grant an absolute reality to phenomena.

Yet, for other people, the ego tends to be indifferent to what appears, it's like it sees nothing. Things are neither comforting nor aggressive nor dangerous. The ego is like the ostrich that seeks out a thick layer of soft, warm sand in order to avoid the world "out there" where things are happening.

Let us return to the example of a beam of light. In this example, the field of vast awareness is reduced in scope to the size of the eye of a needle by identifying with an object that is illuminated.

If this wasn't enough, the ego also believes it is conscious and is proud of this. It's like the frog in "The Frog Who Wished to Be as Big as The Ox" from the Jean De La Fontaine's fable. However, outside of fables, no frog ever had the propensity of the ego to believe that it knew everything.

Thus, within the narrowness of the conscious waking state, the ego feels vulnerable and dependent on phenomena and situations. Consequently, it is in a state of tension which becomes habitual over the course of a lifetime. As such the ego needs to put the final curtain down to tolerate the tensions in daily life.

In conclusion, as long as there is an ego, there are tensions, and as long as there are tensions, sleep is needed. With regard to dreams, one of their main functions is to make painful situations and the contradictions in our behaviors more bearable.

Since the ego cannot cope with these internal contradictions, through dreams, it creates symbolic mediations between what our conscious is able to see and the reality of our emotions.

These are the answers to the question, "Why are sleeping and dreaming so important?"

SYMBOLIC COMMUNICATION OF DREAMS

Even though a large part of the mind is veiled, the narrow conscious sliver still enters into conflict with reality as it is in the course of each day. Meanwhile, to exist, immediate reality doesn't ask the ego for its advice. It exists beyond notions of rejection and acceptance.

As the ego doesn't accept reality as it is, it is in conflict with reality. The ego wants reality to submit itself to its own point of view, which has been conditioned by the ego's past. The ego therefore finds itself in an impossible contradiction that reality shouldn't be what it is.

Each conflict creates additional imprints in the unconscious part of our mind. These imprints persist in our dreams in symbolic forms. In fact, there are two forms of symbols.

One form relates to our personal history. This first form of symbols originates in dualistic grasping and in all the conflicts that have resulted from this grasping. Conflicts have left a mark. In daily life, this residual mark impacts our waking state and dreams in the form of emotions. When they appear to our conscious, we suppress and thus accumulate and maintain them.

The other form of symbols relates to the conflict between our grasped sense of self—the ego—and everything, whether near or far, that relates to purity, emptiness and the sacred. The ego sees these as the end, as death, as the disturbing emptiness or a confusing incomprehensibility.

Symbols are a medium between the narrow and dependent conscious, our grasped personal history, and that which has no limit and is awaiting us when we realize the spiritual goal.

We should therefore take all the above into account in regard to sleep and dreams. We will be able to bring our dreams seriously into account through regular meditation practice and by making progress in non-grasping. Engaging in a serious practice about dreams is useless if as soon as a dream arises, we keep grasping it according to the principles of duality.

COHERENCE AND UNIFYING INTENTION

Through their commitment to observation, intentions, and action, practitioners achieve a coherence that is naturally imbued with benevolence.

Don Quixote was fighting against windmills[30]. Similarly, the ego fights against what belongs to the past, a delusion. In both cases, fighting against what is illusory or past, and using one's intentions and actions to repair what no longer exists can generate contempt, rejection, or benevolence.

Contempt is the rejection of the ego whereas benevolence comes from understanding our behavior. It allows us to see what caused our past behavior and encourages us to return to a wiser understanding.

When a wiser foundation exists, we can stop confusing sleep and rest, and enter a peaceful state through the process of recapitulation (See, *The practice of recapitulation,* page 137), followed by a

---

30 Translator's note, *Don Quixote is a Spanish novel written by Miguel de Cervantes. At some point,* Don Quixote (the main character) believes that windmills are antagonistic giants.

deep relaxation process. Our wish to become aware of our dreams by waking up during the dream phases of the night must be associated with a very deep state of relaxation leading us to sleep.

We practice waking up while dreaming in order to become aware. When we wake up, we begin by expressing our gratitude for still being alive. With respect to life, we see and do everything with a fresh outlook as if for the first time. We are present to the three spheres, and to the awareness that perceive them.

We can then take notes of our dreams. The goal in doing do is not to stimulate our interest or analyze their content but to become aware of the dreamer.

From a contemplative mindset, we don't take notes of what happened, but of the awareness we are, the awareness that perceives what happens. We can write about the awareness we have of our body, of our feelings, and of our mental activity.

During the night, different phases unfold, falling asleep, deep dreamless sleep, and paradoxical sleep with dreams. On average, each night, four phases of deep dreamless sleep alternate with dreaming phases. The stages of sleep occur on four levels. Level four, at the beginning of the night, is the deepest, and level one, in the morning, is the most superficial.

It is not the content of the dream that matters, but the fact of being aware of it. Again, the goal is not to be aware of our dreams. The goal is rather to realize that the awareness we have of our dreams is who we are. We do not have awareness, we are awareness. There is no owner, no appropriation, and nothing to possess. This is the state of non-duality.

Thus, being aware of phenomena is one thing. But being aware that awareness produces and perceives phenomena—in the moment they arise—yet is beyond them. This is what matters. This is what must be realized. This is the goal.

It's a long path that we need to be guided through. It can be dangerous to approach it outside of a rigorous framework. It is also important to get out of the fantasies we usually associate with dreams. Since, here again, we encounter the two usually opposite attitudes of the ego: either a massive disinterest or a neurotic interest in our dreams, that is often exploited by sellers of illusions who pretend to interpret our dreams and take advantage of our credulity to make money.

We remember that our dreams take us back to our history, the way we live our life and what happens in it.

We notice what emerges in our dreams. Do we notice worries, or fears about what we possess, fears about power in regard to our daily ordinary life?

Do we notice spiritual concerns in our dreams? Do we notice big dreams that provide openings? Or are there creative dreams that find their extension in a deeply human daily life?

We observe and ask ourselves these questions, without judging ourselves. We orientate our aspirations and our practices towards the highest direction, in our existence, and beyond it. The connection we establish with a higher purpose is what allows to cross obstacles and catalyze our psycho-physical energies. Let's set up high goals!

The little that has been shared here is not an opinion on the subject, but the succinct result of my more than sixty years' experience. The purpose of this book is to focus on these subjects and to state how important they are. We will return to them in more depth later.

Connecting with spiritual meaning

People who have embarked on an authentic spiritual path demonstrate through their behavior a coherence between their words, their actions, and their mental and emotional state.

This is what we are basically looking for in our current life in which meaning is increasingly difficult to find, and everyone can feel lost. The accumulation of material goods, poverty, suffering, and anguish, that many feel, push us to seek meaning and solutions.

We can't use all the spiritual methods that are available, but it is sufficient to begin our journey towards a more coherent life by using a few or even just one.

Connecting the different phases of our existence and various activities to a spiritual meaning is important. It can unify the idea of our well-being and that of others.

In order to be consistent throughout our life, our sleep, dreams, family life, social life, professional life, birth and death, rest and activity, well-being, and service to others must be connected to a unifying spiritual purpose. We need to check within ourselves if we want these principles to be the foundation for living our life.

These principles have remained valid for 2,500 years, since the time of the Buddha. However, in today's world—when we aren't living a monastic life—we seem to encounter obstacles when applying these principles in our daily life.

In fact, these obstacles are not new. They are inherent to our functioning as human beings. They arise from our dualistic grasping. Any change, be it related to social interactions, our ways of living, family, daily life, suffering, sleep, communication, birth, and death, require adaptation.

Promoting presence and relaxation in daily life

Toning and body-based practices

A good psycho-physical balance in daily life is achieved through practices that tone, energize, relax, stretch, and soften the body. They contribute to our understanding of how the results of our conflicts can accumulate in our body.

Between meditation sessions, practitioners engage in body-based practices associated with breathing practices. These introduce us to meditation practices and relive us from pain and tensions. They untie the subtle energy networks that run through the body.

The practices of self-massage of Kum Nyé (Tibetan Yoga) produces a toning of the body based on the breath and postures during which slow gestures are performed. These practices are complete in themselves. They associate physical movements with the meditative state in order to transmute sensations, emotions and mental contents into their essential nature.

Other practices of Yoga, Tai chi, Qi Gong, and Do In, can also help meditation practices. Physical work has always been a source of balance for people practicing meditation. It is always positive and helpful to alternate the work of the body and that of the mind in our daily life.

Because these practices come from traditional teachings, their goal is beyond duality. They are used to serve our liberation and awakening and not for ego-based outcomes.

Daily relaxation

Deep relaxation, and Shavasana

Entering a state of deep relaxation produces a favorable condition for reminding of the Self and connecting with the sense of awareness. In this context, deep relaxation is not a superficial practice. It has a different intention than the stress-reduction techniques that are often practiced in the West.

Shavasana, also called the "corpse posture", is the name given to a traditional yoga posture in supine position. It is also the name of the state of mind that is actualized in this posture.

When we practice this posture, our sensations are close to the cadaverous state, we feel the sensation that our body has become rigid, heartbeats, respiratory movements, and brain waves decrease, sometimes no longer being detectable at all.

To relax, in prison language, is to be released. In

our daily lives, the ego is a fundamental tension in that it constantly subjects the body to innumerable stresses through the competing energies of desire and aversion.

When we enter into a relaxation process, our mind learns to relax the body. We release our grasping and the egoism investment in this.

As we withdraw our investment in the things of this world, we leave our dependency on them and enter an experience of true being that no longer depends on others' attention nor on what we do in the world. This is the positive emotional aspect of relaxation.

Eventually, the absence of grasping expands and, as in sitting meditation, the Six Dharmas of Tilopa[31] are applied. Mental phenomena are then contemplated from the state of being in which the practitioner is established. In the meditative state, there is no grasping at phenomena since phenomena are perceived as compounded and impermanent. Through this state, they auto-liberate.

The very deep state of relaxation is effectively a meditative state while lying in a horizontal posture. It is useful to point out that the very deep state we reach—without losing consciousness—introduces us to lucidity in sleep, in dreams, as well as at the time of death. Very deep relaxation requires intensive practice. As such this state is rarely achieved.

In the exposition of the nine methods for stabilizing the mind described in the *Ocean of*

---

31 Tilopa is a great Tibetan yogi, one of the great masters of the Kagyu lineage. In the "*Six Nails of key points*», he defines the state that practitioners must actualize in meditation: "Don't reflect. Don't imagine. Don't think. Don't meditate. Don't analyze. Remain within yourself." (*Ocean of Certainty*, 9th Karmapa).

Certainty, the ninth point is to "Remain calm." The text says, "It is no longer possible to be distracted, whether one is meditating or not. Meditation is no longer interrupted." This means that we remain undistracted in every moment, during sleep, rest, and other activities.

In this deep state of relaxion or meditation, several steps are taken. Our mind is firstly oriented towards the process of deepening relaxation and concentration. Then, we use the relaxed and focused state to develop our aspiration to reach the ultimate goal. Finally, we use the reminding of the Self and the sense of awareness. As a result, once we are out of our formal practice, whatever daily life activity we engage in, from the non-conscious part of the self where the seed was planted, the reminder occurs in the conscious part of the mind.

Our aspiration persists, our relaxed state persists, their effects persist, our state of awareness persists, and this allows our aspiration, the practice, and its ultimate meaning to be seeded again and again. We need to be introduced and guided through the details of this whole process and then diligently practice it.

Although the ultimate level can bring many positive results to our life, still this experience of a profound uninterrupted relaxation is difficult to achieve. If we train seriously, we can begin to notice many benefits. As we become more relaxed in our body, and more aware, the physiological and psychological effects allow us to rest more deeply, and this translates into increased energy to carry out our daily activities.

As our state of presence improves, our awareness of situations and of our own sense of self produces a great saving of psycho-physical energy. This is due to having a better perception of the meaning of reality, a clearer vision of the actions we need to perform, and a greater sense of adequacy in terms of achieving results.

The fact that we see things in their reality with more accuracy and precision leads to a drastic reduction in the number of conflicts we encounter, both small and large. Then, the inner critic that constantly runs throughout our life: "I should have...", "It should have been like this...", "This isn't possible!", "It's not true!!!" etc. progressively diminishes.

Disposition of the mind in everyday life

Reminding of the Self, and reminding of the profound meaning

Traditionally, practitioners listen to the teachings, then reflect on them and finally practice them. If they find them to be true and beneficial for themselves and others, they continue with the practice.

We previously explained why it is important to not get caught in everything that happens in our environment and how remaining present to our existence and its profound meaning is essential.

This is where we'll start. We should carry a profound meaning [?] within us. When circumstances or teachings seem right to us, even if we learn something from them, it doesn't mean that we will take them further.

We should think about the teachings. But we shouldn't believe that we are applying them and taking them further just by understanding them intellectually or being convinced by them. When we agree with a teaching, when it sounds accurate, important, and meaningful to us, a whole process of integration begins.

This process is traditionally broken down into nine stages of progression which include lower, middle, and higher levels of understanding; lower, middle, and higher experiences; and lower, middle and higher realizations. We should use this progression as a reference. However, the ego operates differently. As soon as it understands something intellectually, the ego believes it possesses it and is capable of fully accomplishing it. For most of us this is wrong.

After listening to a teaching, the first step consists of thinking about it again and again. We find examples within our own experience and break them down using logic and analysis until we reach some level of certainty (for example, we reflect about our experience of impermanence).

Then, we start integrating the meaning of the teaching and become really able to use it when circumstances require. To do this, a reminder is needed. We call this, "reminding the self, accompanied by reminding the profound meaning". To be complete, the reminder should include "the three spheres" (See, *Domain of ego extension*, page 25) namely the self, other, and the division between the two.

When we talk about the reminding of the Self, this doesn't imply grasping at a self, a "me" as an independent entity. Rather we remind ourselves of a sense of Self that exists beyond grasping itself[32].

Often, it's because of the suffering we experience in our life, that we embark on an inner journey. In order to progress, we lean on suffering.

Over time, we can progress in establishing deeper levels of understanding, levels of realization that gradually modify the conception we have of ourselves.

When we grasp the ultimate meaning of our existence and realize the profound intention in this life, we begin practicing diligently and without any distractions. In this way we gradually purify ourselves of egocentric grasping.

In reminding the Self, and the profound meaning, in a way, we don't do anything. Our intention comes back to us as a positive imprint. We become aware of our tactile sensations. Focusing on our tactile sensation makes us present to whatever arises, within ourselves or outside our body envelop, and ultimately present to the awareness that perceives this tactile sensation.

From a state of observation that is free of all grasping, we use our tactile sensation (which reminds us of spaciousness and awareness itself) to recall our intention. And each time we remember our intention, we take this opportunity to renew it.

By renewing our intention on many occasions, our actions are more easily oriented towards the achievement of our intention. We stay on course, so to speak. Rather than wasting our time in fruitless actions, we fully devote ourselves to our goal.

---

32   In this instance, Self is written with a capital S, to refer to the liberating potential inherent in the ungrasped individuality endowed with precious human existence. In Buddhism, human existence is considered precious, free and well-endowed because our human life enables us to realize the nature of mind.

For our precious human existence to be meaningful we must first determine that meaning and seed it. Then, we must remember it, as frequently as possible, so that we don't lose our direction along the way.

Our ultimate intention is the main dynamic that underlies our whole life. The reminders of this intention allow us to direct all our actions towards this direction.

This meaning can, for example, aim for unity with others or altruism. In this case, we devote our actions to altruism. And we remember our intention, we repeat it internally. Tactile sensations help us renew our intention on multiple occasions throughout the day.

By doing so, by repeating our intentions, by remembering them—instantly—and many times over, we progress, step by step, toward our ultimate goal.

In the reminding of the Self, we create a linkage to the tactile sensation in the present moment and use this connection as a support. It is a means of remembering pure awareness, the spacelike nature of the mind. The unobstructed spacelike awareness exists in a permanent moment-to-moment renewal. Our tactile sensation is therefore a reliable support in that it objectifies the present state of awareness in its momentary existence.

Everything that has just been explained must be understood, then reflected upon and updated throughout our life. How? As previously indicated, any in-depth integration will depend initially on the conditions. In addition to practitioners' capacity to understand the teachings intellectually and their capacity to reflect on their meaning, they must be able to enter a deeply relaxed state, a concentrated state, and a positive emotional state. These need to be accessed repeatedly, over time. These are the conditions that need to come together to actualize the reminder of the profound meaning we carry with us.

The above could be summed up in the following formula, "seeing, being determined, being able, and accomplishing."

We must see something a hundred times to develop a true drive, a real determination. This is the only way to overcome the obstacle of ego grasping. Then it takes a hundred determinations to reach the ability to act. A hundred abilities are finally necessary to become able to accomplish and achieve.

We should therefore reach a state of deep relaxation and focus on the goal of the reminder when making an aspiration, a simply formulated resolution, and do this several times. We should do it with faith and confidence, in a state of devotion towards the ultimate goal.

We should also rely on the relaxed and very aware state of our sense of self in relationship with our tactile sensation to formulate the aspiration to remember the Self and the profound meaning throughout the various moments of our daily life. The tactile sensation is a support of attention, not a support of concentration. It isn't what the ego perceives as the place that objectifies the division between awareness and space. To the contrary, the tactile sensation is the precise place where the unity between exterior and interior is experienced.

The place where we feel the tactile sensation therefore becomes the symbolic place in which awareness which perceives without grasping is revealed in its momentariness: a past body as well as a future body cannot be "felt". The tactile sensation is the sign of the immediacy of the body, and of the immediacy of the awareness that perceives it.

Likewise, the bodily envelope felt through tactile sensations is insubstantial and doesn't separate an interior from an exterior. This way we free ourselves from our aberrant grasping of a division between self and other.

The unified attention encompassing what is usually split into inner space, outer space, and the division between these two is called "beyond the three spheres".

Do not create an opposition between the sacred and the profane

As we keep saying, the ego's principle is division. It divides, then subdivides, ad infinitum, in all circumstances. The opposition between sacred and profane is by far the most painful division. It has fueled so many conflicts over the centuries, in many countries, across all cultures and all races.

Too often, the ego has used its power and thirst for possessions under the guise of religion.

The role of the spiritual dimension is to generate benevolence, openness, and tolerance. This must be established in ourselves, then in our daily life and within our practice.

We shouldn't reduce ourselves to the negative actions we have committed in the past. We should develop the intention to do good for ourselves and for others. We should rely on our potential and on the continual freshness of the moment. Both allow us to influence our behavior in the present moment, today and tomorrow.

We shouldn't see the world and others as the cause of our suffering but realize that it is our ego that brings unhappiness to the world and hardship to our lives.

Disposition to practice meditation

A FRESH APPROACH TO LIFE

In order to practice meditation correctly, we need to stop complaining about things and develop within ourselves qualities such as humility, clear and undistorted vision, love, and equanimity.

When we habitually magnify the slightest obstacle, the slightest discomfort, and when our usual mode of functioning produces paranoia or fantasy, our practices as well as our daily life circumstances will be deformed by our projections.

What we aim for is to see phenomena as phenomena, without bias, free from the distorting mirror of our personal history.

Attention without grasping is the only way to abandon conditioned interpretations about external or internal phenomena. This type of attention also frees us up from doubt, rejection, and attachment, as well as ignorance.

SIMPLY SEEING

When we are meant to observe, we shouldn't do anything else. Our immediate reality is made up of basic facts—things, what happens, what is, thoughts, emotions, reality, etc. There is nothing to look for and nothing to reject or interpret, we should just see things as they are, and not as our ego would like them to be.

We see what happens, and we become aware of what is, as if we were a neutral witness, with an equanimous way of seeing, without interpreting.

Awareness is present in every moment whether there are phenomena or not. If a phenomenon occurs, it is a basic fact. If we see it, it is right. To reject or accept it, isn't right by nature. Facts are an immediate reality and immediate reality doesn't ask for our opinion in order to manifest itself as it is. Immediate reality is therefore beyond rejection and acceptance.

In the field of awareness, which is the nature of the mind, everything manifests. There is nothing outside of this field, either in terms of the faculties producing phenomena or the perception of them.

We should notice that our focus of attention is strongly tainted by dualistic ego-grasping. Our attention is dependent on what arises, either outside or inside. It is given to phenomena without free choice. Pleasant or unpleasant phenomena capture our attention. The more unpleasant or painful they are, the more attractive power they have.

FREE OF GRASPING

As practitioners, as human beings, we should protect our awareness, and our existence from the enslavement of ego-grasping. Grasping is what seals our dependency on phenomena. Healing from our enslavement is essential.

When we meditate, if a mental phenomenon arises and is attractive, we grasp it, and become absorbed in it. We cease being aware of the pure awareness we are.

Submitting our minds to what they produce is equivalent to making human beings dependent on the robots they create. We should not allow that to happen.

We seek to experience a sense of being through phenomena. This is why we want phenomena to be solid and lasting, and absolutely existent. A consequence of this automatic grasping is that we proclaim ownership over what we perceive, especially when it corresponds to what the ego wants or expects.

When the experience of our own existence is dependent on phenomena, every time something disappears, which is inevitable, it is as if we were disappearing with it. Furthermore, our suffering is compounded because we attributed an absolute nature to everything that comes and goes. This perpetuates the grief we experience when we lose someone or something we were very attached to, a relative, our job, our home or our country.

When we believe that phenomenon have an absolute reality[33], that they exist from their own side, we see them as being the source of our happiness. In order to regain a feeling of unity, which is actually illusory, we try to possess phenomena. We are like children who believe in Santa Claus or who cannot live without their comfort blanket.

---

33 The ego grasps phenomena as uncompounded, self-existing units. It sees them as unrelated to other things.

We thus prepare ourselves for future suffering. The Buddha said to his first disciples: "I will teach you only about suffering, the cause of suffering, happiness, and the path to it".

We might think that teaching about suffering and its root cause is unnecessary. Yet even when we talk about spiritual practices and begin to implement them, whether in our daily actions or in our formal practice, we almost immediately turn to talking about obstacles and difficulties.

By holding onto obstacles, we make them solid and durable. Our unconscious tendencies have a habit of focusing on what is negative. We also try to recreate an exact representation of the world with which we are familiar and don't want to leave. The world is like a worn coat that we are very attached to and won't throw out.

In order to be alive and happy, as practitioners we should turn towards happiness and move away from the world of habits.

We impute an absolute reality to the self, to others, and to the division between them. As a result, disturbing emotions arise following our tendencies. We then grasp these as obstacles, along with their innumerable consequences.

It's like thinking that butter exists, has always existed, and will always exist. We believe that butter exists in itself, that butter doesn't come from milk, nor the milk from a cow, etc.

It's like thinking that butter itself is contained in its name and believing that this name has existed forever.

Although we can be aware, this seems to be the most difficult thing in the world to realize. However, when a mental phenomenon arises, there is a consciousness that produces and perceives it.

We should reflect on and then implement these different points in our meditation practice and daily life.

We must stop grasping at obstacles. We begin by noticing our grasping. Then we need to realize that there is no time for being absent and wasting our precious existence in this body.

The extreme limit of non-existence consists of looking at the past—which no longer exists—and identifying with it, then projecting a future—that doesn't exist either—based on that past.

THE HERE AND NOW

All Dharma [Buddha's teaching, and journey or way to enlightenment] depends on the mind, and the mind depends on intentions. The intention is therefore important: "Through listening and reflection, may I achieve enlightenment and establish therein all beings who have been our mothers"[34].

If we seek to determine where phenomena, all inner or outer manifestations occur, there is only one answer, in the here and now.

It doesn't matter whether they are emotions connected to our past or projections towards the future, they manifest themselves in our mind, right here in this very moment.

Because we identify with these impressions, they veil our mind which is still present and perceives them. If we could recognize the presence of the mind itself—who we really are—we would be free

---

34   This is how we should conceive all sentient beings, as our own mother.

from attachment to impressions that are all relative. We would then be established in the state that is unaffected and free of all reactivity.

Our link with the present already exists, we don't need to create it. Like the drawings on a tapestry pattern, we just have to follow them to easily complete the embroidery.

THE SUPPORT OF ATTENTION

That's how it happens in Shine[35] when we choose a support of attention. The support of attention helps us to not following phenomena, while neither rejecting them nor becoming unaware of them.

Establishing a connection with a support of attention is not trivial. In this we are already stepping out of our dependence on phenomena. This is the first step towards free will. Nothing is more important than this first step on our path to freedom and happiness.

The connection with the support—which is renewed in every moment—is in fact the connection to the immediacy of the moment. It is "being present".

Phenomena arise in the present. Being connected with the support is therefore being at the root of the manifestations, which is where we need to be to achieve the goal of meditation.

The state of presence doesn't need to be created; it already exists. The state of presence is that of pure awareness, the nature of the mind. The support of attention brings us closer to this state, as we establish the connection in a subtle way.

---

35 Shine or "zhinay": "shi" means tranquil, calming, "ne" means abiding. In meditation practice, it is the base from which higher vision can be exercised.

Establishing the connection with the support brings together the following competencies:

(1) We become truly capable of choosing. We are able to place our attention consciously and voluntarily on an object and return to it whenever necessary.

(2) We establish ourselves in the present moment, which means to experience life as only this moment.

(3) We eliminate the functioning of the ego—the process of grasping, rejecting, or being unconscious of phenomena in the present moment.

(4) We abandon partiality.

(5) We let go of judgment.

(6) We remove desire.

(7) We eradicate ignorance.

(8) We let go of doubt and feelings of incapacity.

The last five capacities are signs that the transmutation of our unconscious negative tendencies has already begun.

GENTLY COMING BACK

The natural state of our mind is its presence. Like the tapestry pattern mentioned above, the instructions on meditation practice simply reveal the state of presence. They reveal the already present jewel.

We just need to introduce the needle wherever it is appropriate in the weft thread, follow the pre-traced design and admire how a somewhat dull drawing becomes luminous when the colored thread gives it some relief.

We can admire how relative reality becomes luminous when presence and awareness are woven into it and illuminate it.

The consciously and voluntarily established connection with the support brings us into continuous synchronicity with the present moment, from one, moment to the next. It requires a constant interest, and an enthusiastic warmth. When a phenomenon arises, our interest and enthusiasm help us in not following it, not pushing it away and not ignoring it. Lukewarm interest will not suffice. Freedom and life deserve enthusiasm!

We shouldn't spend and waste our time fighting so called distractions, we are distracted. This proves that phenomena have power over the ego. We shouldn't resign ourselves to ignoring the being we are.

As long as we think that happiness or unhappiness depends on the outside, on what is happening in the world, we can only be subjected to the conditioned state.

When we place our attention on a support, if it is "really" placed, our mind doesn't seek anything. It doesn't question itself. It doesn't comment on anything. There is nothing to say, nothing to tell ourselves, we simply perceive.

When we first try to do this, we realize that we spend most of our time commenting about the world. The elimination of such a habit will take a long time because our very existence depends on the dynamic unconscious production of phenomena. Indeed, for the ego, there must be phenomena. When none are occurring outside, the ego produces internal events.

When we become aware that we have let ourselves be carried away by external or internal phenomena, we should bring the mind back to the support, gently, slowly, without any negative comments, even subtle ones. This gentleness is traditionally compared to that of the mahout towards the elephant which, tied to the stake, doesn't even pull on the rope.

Improving our State

Shiné teaches us non-grasping. It reduces the interactions in the mind and thereby the number of mental phenomena.

The mind consequently becomes clearer. Tranquility and clarity increase. Results are only slow to manifest when a practitioner doesn't apply the instructions precisely.

To enter a virtuous dynamic, we should extend the principles of meditation to our daily life. As our grasping diminishes, it becomes clear that the hustle and bustle of everyday life is a source of suffering. It is then no longer sought after or maintained. This, of course, doesn't mean that one becomes inactive.

Shine provides access to three experiences, stability, clarity, and bliss. It establishes a foundation for Lhaktong—the state of higher vision. This is the reason why we should never abandon the practice of shine.

Why do we associate Shine with clarity? When we begin the practice of Shine, we can easily mistake a state of torpor or opacity with a state of tranquility. And under the veil of torpor, a great restlessness might still exist.

This is why clarity is essential. Being peaceful and remaining peaceful for a long time requires a clear, hence unveiled, mind.

The implementation of our meditation practice should include the events and experiences that have reinforced our restlessness throughout our personal life, as these will shape the various difficulties we encounter in our practice.

When we practice Shine, we can count the number of respiratory cycles. A cycle is composed of three phases:

(1) The inspiration
(2) The moment of equilibrium and
(3) The exhalation

If we are following our breath, we count from 1 to 21 for one cycle. When we become distracted, we start again from 1.

In another form of Shine—called "recitation meditation"—each of the breathing phases is associated with one seed syllable from the mantra, "om ah hum". In this method, we associate "om"— the manifested world we perceive—with the inspiration; "ah"—the dynamics participating in its manifestation—with the moment of equilibrium; and "hum"—the nature of the mind, emptiness— with the exhalation.

We practice this method, day and night throughout all our activities[36], with the aspiration to remember emptiness, the dynamics of wisdom and the manifestation as a whole.

Our relationship to the world, our communication with those around us, particularly when we were a child, may have contributed to our shortcomings, fears, and needs for compensation. All this is to be considered in order to improve our state.

---

36 Activities: work, meals, leisure, sleep, dreams, etc.

Considerations on communication and ways to improve it

Good relationships with others can only be envisaged by considering the interdependence that exists between all the elements involved in a holistic dynamic. This includes sentient beings, their conscious and unconscious relationships, their education, the repressed elements of their emotional life as well as the play of their unconscious tendencies.

If we consider communication in its global aspect, observation shows that when there is conflict between us and the world around us, the division we feel ranges throughout our interior space.

The impact of this division is immediate. It first affects our ego mind, then the emotional layer of our sense of self and finally our body through the endocrine system.

These three layers are called the "koshas" in Sanskrit, meaning layers or sheaths. They mainly interact in five different locations, from the mental layer, passing through the emotional layer, to the physical layer.

At the mental level, the locations of these functions correspond to what's called "chakras" in Sanskrit, which means wheel. At the emotional level, interactions happen within the plexuses. And at the physical level, they happen with the endocrine glands which influence all our gross physiology.

On a general level, we should be aware that communication is not only established between two or more people. Within an individual, communication also exists between the conscious and unconscious aspects. This communication happens in both directions.

For example, if we think of the notions of a seed and reminder, when a practitioner formulates an aspiration to wake up during the dream phase of sleep, and they do indeed wake up, they can then notice that their aspiration generated the result. The veiled part of their mind is no longer an obstacle, but the soil for unification.

When we become conscious of a dream, the conscious aspect of ourselves notes it. The act of noting it is the manifest sign of the reunification of our conscious and unconscious.

Communication should also be understood as verbal and non-verbal. It must also be reciprocal, balanced between self and other, between conscious and unconscious and vice versa. Too often, we hear journalists or politicians asking questions without waiting for answers to ask further questions, which only increases the animosity between the interlocutors. Verbal violence that underlies ego dynamics thus becomes a system to seduce their audience.

Through arts and cultural activities, there is communication between artists who paint, sculpt, or sing, for example, and those who come to see their creation or hear them perform.

Just one of these acts of communication is not enough. To communicate we must try to both understand and be understood. When there is no equanimity between expression and understanding, when genuine interest in the other is lacking, there is no communication.

Interdependence between different types of communication

Dualistic grasping is the cause of the division between our conscious and unconscious. In the same way, the accumulation of conflicts further reduces the space of what we called the "conscious". Consequently, for most people what arises at first from the unconscious part of the mind is what we reject. Most of the time, it appears in a symbolic form.

Communication between the conscious and unconscious parts of our mind is necessary. Each part should have a chance to express itself and be heard by the other one.

Both parts often express themselves in a strong, or even aggressive way, as minorities who have been ignored for a long time. Our conscious part mainly expresses itself through reactions of fear and worry, which reinforces the feeling of division.

For example, in a nightmare, if we feel pursued by a monster, we identify with a small part of our self, a part we call "me". This part is pursued by a monster that we experience as "other". The pursuit occurs in a specific context with objects, other characters, and an environment. We are afraid of the monster, and its apparent aggression when, in reality, our own mind produces it. Our own mind also produces the small part we identify with as "me". Rejection produces persistence and perpetuation of the ego throughout our lives.

One part of the mind has something to say to the other, which doesn't hear it, often for a long time, perhaps because it cannot. It is up to the practitioner to understand this and develop a mediating intention.

The simple fact that the practitioner understands it in the waking state, that she learns through meditation not to grasp, is a good disposition for the communication to be established.

In popular wisdom, such a disposition has been known for a long time. When loving parents tell their children terrifying tales at bedtime, they introduce the disposition for courage, non-grasping and to all the qualities of a brave knight who copes.

Throughout our life, we learn to cope, to reduce our grasping, and to integrate fear. We must respect our own pace in gaining confidence and finding support. Competent people might help us, but it also takes practice and method.

Symptoms of the division between us and others will only grow stronger if we push them away in different ways. Therefore, learning meditation practice is very useful. It teaches us to cope and stop grasping. Phenomena that arise in our mind should be approached with our attention and not through a mental activity that is partial, because it is conditioned.

The conscious component misunderstands the language of our unconscious part, whether it is expressed in the form of symbolic imagery, in dreams, or in the form of emotions or symptoms of a psychic origin. Nevertheless, the unconscious part needs to express itself. Covering it up, pushing it away, wanting it to disappear without hearing what it is expressing are not good solutions.

Meditation practices, associated with daily life attention and consideration of the above, are means to pacify us. Of course, we need to adapt them to according to people's predispositions.

UNIFIED VISION OF DIFFERENT TYPES OF COMMUNICATION

All of the topics in this book are interrelated. In this universe, everything is in interaction. No individual can be separated from her or his essence, nor from phenomena, or other beings.

Despite the compartmentalization of experience orchestrated by the ego, the emotions we experience in our daily lives have repercussions on our sleep, our dreams, our breathing, and our way of eating and digesting.

This introductory book aims to bring a unified vision to the different times and activities of our daily life. This is why the topic of communication is important. In order to avoid the accumulation of the negative effects that can build up in every area of our daily life, we must become aware of the various interdependencies at play.

Nothing that happens in the small area of the mind that we call "conscious" is separate from the veiled field of awareness, which we don't recognize. Whether inside or beyond the sense of self we wrongly call "me", nothing is independent of the field and all compounded phenomena. There is no owner because everything that is composed sooner or later will returns to its essence. Nothing that happens in this immense and unrecognized field is really separated from the so-called "conscious" part.

The ego is like an authoritarian person. The ego classifies, categorizes, judges, names, and explains the workings of the world. It doesn't like contradictions. It also needs certainty. It expects to find the world of the next moment as it left it the moment before.

This dictator-jailer gives itself the power to make laws. It prevents progress and life, blocks the natural function of communication between the parts that should always communicate with each other, since that is their natural state.

My fifty years' experience in providing counseling support has shown me that relational problems and communication difficulties appear at all levels.

Communication difficulties appear in all situations, between individuals, but also between conscious and subconscious[37] and between subconscious and conscious. For example, when providing counseling support, I often notice that the conscious part of people's mind refuses to be confronted with itself— with manifestations of the subconscious part, which could nonetheless be illuminating. People generally don't even speak about their subconscious, neither to me as their counselor nor to anyone else. Yet talking about it would support their progress.

The blockage of communication we may have with someone is often an expression of the conflict or miscommunication between our conscious and subconscious which aren't communicating with each other.

This is why in counseling we open up new possibilities by facilitating the communication between these two parts. Having opened up new possibilities, we then transform them to their fulfilment. There are several practices that can promote a communicative state of mind and restore the channels of communication broken by our conditioning habits.

---

37 Again, the term "subconscious" seems more appropriate than the "unconscious" to represent what awareness is, which is ever present although veiled, just as phenomena, which are also veiled.

A few years back, a study showed that what a large majority of people regretted the most in their lives was not having told their parents that they loved them before their death.

This shows us how positive feelings that aren't expressed, for whatever reason, can become disturbing emotions. Therefore, parents should encourage their children to express their feelings and emotions. This doesn't mean that we shouldn't set limits. But in setting them, we should explain to children why we set these limits and let them know that these limits don't call into question the love we have for them.

Another important point, when conflicts cannot be expressed and resolved, they leave an imprint that will inhibit communication in the future and impair our capacity to solve life difficulties and grieve. It is therefore essential to show courage and benevolence by doing everything we can to quickly connect with people with whom we are in conflict and strive to resolve our issues. On the other hand, dwelling on our resentment and pouring it out years later must be absolutely avoided because it is futile and often disproportionate.

Sometimes we use the term "good communicators" to refer to people who can explain things well. But, in the same way that knowing is not understanding, "explaining" shouldn't be confused with "expressing".

Similarly, believing that we are expressing ourselves when we let ourselves get carried away by our emotions is a very narrow way of understanding communication.

Communication presupposes a willingness to understand others and to therefore listen to them. It also implies explaining and expressing ourselves in ways that can be understood by others.

Communicating doesn't mean crushing others with emotional responses as a way of refusing to listen to them.

In recent decades it has become popular for universities and businesses to study how people show love, care and interest in others. They have analysed people's gestures, behaviors, and listening patterns and transformed these into systems that mimic the apparent signs of attention and care. These techniques are now taught in management schools and in businesses to increase the effectiveness of marketing and promote profits.

Yet, when we are genuinely interested in others, all the signs of authentic and loving communication are present without needing to fabricate them. Authentic communication isn't based on techniques.

Communication, in its various aspects, depends on "Maitri", which means, benevolence or loving-kindness. Communications skills are balanced with interpersonal skills. Using one without the other ultimately produces unbalanced outcomes.

In everyday life for example, in order for verbal communication to be balanced, we should express both the thoughts and feelings we experience. Most of the time, only one of these is expressed.

Too often, we witness deaf dialogues. Someone expresses their emotions, loading their words with emotions in front of someone else who responds with thought, loading their communication with reasons.

This is reflected in the formula, "Tell me what you *need*. And I will *explain* how to do without it."

For communication to be effective, we need to

be aware, in the moment, of ourselves and these we are communicating with. When expressing our emotions, we need to be aware of what the other person can receive. We express, then explain. Being aware of the other, when we express some reasoning thoughts, we should temper our explanations by expressing our feelings, while also paying attention to, and including, the other person.

When we communicate through speech, our words should be adapted to include what we have to say according to the capacities and understanding of the listener.

When we feel love[38] and benevolence, attention and inclusion are naturally present in our communication.

Let's now look at spoken language, although we have heard and learnt a large number of words and expressions from our early childhood, the language we use on a daily basis is, in general, extremely restrained and stereotyped.

The less creative we are, the more the phenomenal world impacts on us. When General de Gaulle used the term "chienlit"[39] in one of his speeches, everyone opened their dictionary, even the journalists

Nowadays, a day can't go by without hearing formula like, "It's amazing!" At one end, a cultured man of power uses formulas knowing the effect his words can produce; and at the other hand, less creative and less cultured people only repeat expressions that don't mean much.

---

38 Love is an altruistic feeling that expects nothing in return, unlike desire-attachment that seeks to possess the other.

39 Translator's note, in 1968, "chienlit", which means "havoc", was an expression unknown to the general public in France.

Of course, our behavior, gestures, postures, and our facial expressions participate in our communication. We should be aware of these, because often simply raising our eyebrows or shrugging can trigger someone's anger.

Our postures, gestures, all postural language are also forms of expression. As a baby, we learnt facial expressions from our mother's face[40] and memorized them during our dreams. These mainly define the range of expressions of feelings and emotions that we will use throughout our lives. For each form of expression (mental, verbal, written, postural, gestural) a large potential of variations exists. The full range of expressions is far broader than the ones we use, which are shaped in habits and conditioning.

Basically, we should realize that we are conditioned[41] and that our expression is ritualized at every level. For people who are radically opposed to rituals, noticing how ritually they are opposed to them, may help them progress in broadening their conceptions. This is true for all of us.

If we were filmed when we enter our room each evening, when we go to bed, we'd notice all the rituals we perform on a daily basis. The way we get undressed; how we store or our clothes or just put them in a pile; which part of the bed we lie down in, the position we assume, etc. Most of our gestures are ritualized. This is true of most of our daily activities.

We can choose between confining and unconscious

---

40 Facial expressions : babies learn this emotional language in their visual relationship with their mothers and engram them for their whole life.

41 Professor Laborit [French surgeon, neurobiologist, philosopher, and author], and his work have demonstrated how conditioned we are. See the movie, "*My American Uncle*" by Alain Resnais.

rituals, oriented towards aggressiveness, violence and our ego, or conscious and voluntary rituals, oriented towards progress, the good for others, suffused with benevolence.

As we make progress in our practice, we become aware of what arises in our mind, in terms of habitual interpretations of the world, which determines our interactions with it, including the ways and forms through which we express ourselves. We see how everything is interconnected and interdependent. We begin to question whether we are free and creative or dependent and conditioned. Are we able to change, and innovate, or do we relinquish our potential every day?

Rumination

This book doesn't offer a detailed analysis of the individual psychology of the different tendencies related to our sense of self. Here, it is enough to say that one of the five fundamental tendencies dominates in our mind. On this conditioned foundation, our ego therefore interprets what is happening moment by moment.

The Karma tendency that leads to rumination is characterized by difficulty in choosing, needing to make comparisons, feelings of doubt and abandonment, a sense of devaluation, and a strong dependence the judgment and approval of others.

A lot of our inner life is spent in rumination. We ruminate about events that have a basis in early conditioning, memories that have been knitted into our childhood experience. We also ruminate about specific events that have happened in the recent past. For example, being destabilized, suffering an injustice, can induce this form of mental agitation. This agitation can add to the interplay of the fundamental tendencies in their negative aspect.

This agitation or restlessness disrupts our sleep and promotes insomnia. It is exhausting. It contributes to the development of anxiety or depression. It is therefore important, though not necessarily easy, to treat agitation quickly, so that it doesn't become a habitual condition.

Indeed, it is always more difficult to change a behavior that has become, as we say, "second nature". When we rehash the past, it means that the Karma tendency of our mind is at work, in its negative aspect, no matter what has triggered our rehashing.

The Karma tendency—activity—easily explains the game of ping-pong that begins in the mind and repeats itself on many circumstances, again and again. This recurring aspect should be noticed and used as a switch to cut the root of the negative processes that are involved.

Indeed, we should not pay attention to the object of our thoughts, as such, but rather to the fact that we are attached to the objects of our thinking, [be they people, inanimate phenomena, feelings, or other thoughts.] It is training in meditation that allows us to abandon our grasping, and which will eventually let us detach ourselves from rumination.

While we are developing the capacity to let go of our grasping, as we become aware of it, it can be useful to employ a breathing technique, or a form of practice of attention to the body to help us detach from reprocessing the past.

If these aren't sufficient, we may need some help in finding and expressing the causes of our agitation. Because a negative tendency is not so easy to transmute, we should continue to take care of our own mental hygiene at the same time.

When an event impacts our mind, it destabilizes us, it generates self-doubt and doubt about others. Our self-image is affected.

For the Karma tendency, recovering a positive self-image, is always linked to others' attention, and the fear of being abandoned, both literally and figuratively.

The feeling of abandonment can be a major element of the process of needing to rehash the past. An action or an idea arises in order to answer a given situation. Then doubt emerges, then the comparison between this idea and another, or between oneself and others is reinforced.

Once this process has been set off, it becomes tighter, narrower, with many interactions, like a snake biting its tail.

When the wind of emotion has risen, it becomes difficult to calm it down. From one interaction, another arises. These endless sequences leave no room for reasoning. The mind becomes like a runaway horse.

Regaining self-confidence and a more noble vision of ourselves can imply receiving help from a good friend or a counsellor who is not involved in our personal history. We need the courage to share our difficulties and sufferings with someone we trust, who shows us kind attention.

We need the discipline, courage, and perseverance to confront our vulnerabilities with attention and wisdom. This is what will allow us to recover our sense of self-worth.

Very often, what would be useful isn't done or even begun. An idea doesn't even have time to form, before another idea displaces it, pulling the rug from under a potentially useful idea. The end result is that no choice is made, no useful action is accomplished.

It is essential to understand this cycle, where one thought is displaced by another unrelated thought leading us to being ineffectual, which damages our self-esteem. We need to recognize the early symptoms of this "circus"[42] in our mind.

We need to understand the process involved when we lose focus, become inefficient, which result in a loss of self-confidence. This mechanism is behind rehashing. The main reason we succumb to rehashing is that the ego—because it has understood the process intellectually—believes that understanding is enough to become capable and change. My experience has repeatedly shown me that only a few people succeed at modifying this pattern.

Once we see this cycle happening, we can immediately engage in a mental practice. This doesn't consist of trying to stop anything happening. Rather we harness the energy of the wind which previously threw us off course. And use the strength of the wind energy to reorient our mind in a useful direction of accomplishment instead of feeding self-doubt and stagnation.

---

42 "Circus" here refers to disordered mental activity, which goes around in circles, where each new thought causes the previous one to fall into oblivion.

What practice should we adopt? The best is either a method of attention to the body[43] or the use of a mantra which require transmission from an instructor. The use of a vigorous and active body practice can also help calm the agitation of wind[44].

Finally, no practice should be set up in opposition to obstacles. We should fervently turn our mind towards the positive goal that includes working for the welfare of others.

Using a practice as a means of rejecting phenomena, which we arbitrarily considered as defaults, shows us that there is judgment, which is conditioned by the past. Our practice is then directed towards the past instead of being focused on the present moment with the goal of actualizing what is beneficial.

This concealed repulsion not only reinforces what we reject, it also contributes to losing our confidence in the practice, since we attribute any negative result

---

43 When talking about a method of attention to the body, we refer not to the notion of a solid body, but to an insubstantial, uncompounded body, that has no intrinsic existence.

44 In terms of energy, the wind, the air element is linked to the Karma dynamics. When the wind element is in excess, it is necessary to make it more peaceful and serene.

This wind dynamic is linked to activity, in all its forms, emotional, physical, and mental. In its wisdom aspect—the accomplishing wisdom—the wind element is the energy that allow things to circulate, the energy that mixes them together, it is what's generates movement.

The wisdom aspect is the capacity to use causes and consequences towards accomplishment instead of being outflanked by them.

Once the wind element is mastered, the nature of mind is able to contemplate and use the energy of the wind rather than being carried away by the movement or being dependent on it.

The Ratna energy is associated to the earth element.

The Vajra energy is associated to the water element.

The Padma energy is associated to the fire element.

The Buddha energy is associated to the space element.

Earth, water, air, fire are all contained in the space element. None of these elements can exist without space. None of the elements can exist without all of the other ones. They all are interdependent.

to the practice itself. Whereas in fact the negative result only stems from our misunderstanding. This is an extremely common distortion in daily life as well as in spiritual practice.

This is a form of attachment we need to eradicate. The object of our attachment is not the problem itself, but our dependence on the objects of attachment which only exists in our mind. Therefore, it's our mindset that we need to change.

The ego is an extremist, it is only concerned with its own existence. The ego wants to bend the world to its own point of view, since this is what it is attached to. Love itself embraces all, without any expectation.

RECAPITULATION

When we have developed a solid base of meditation practice, it is also good to practice recapitulation. (See, *The practice of recapitulation,* page 137)

When we are not yet seasoned meditators, we can be at risk of grasping a sequence of recapitulation, in which case, recapitulation only produces agitation.

Note, however, that voluntarily and consciously observing our mental contents doesn't necessarily mean being overtaken by them. Facing up to what we notice, at whatever level we are capable, is a path to tranquility and increases confidence.

Sleep and dreams

We spend a third of our life sleeping and a quarter of our sleep time dreaming. When we reach sixty, we have therefore spent twenty years sleeping and five years dreaming.

Any other activity, carried out with such regularity and for such a long time, would generate a lot of interest and questions. This is rarely the case for sleep and dreams. We are only interested in sleep when it is disturbed. And we mainly limit our attention to dreams when disturbing nightmares wake us.

Moreover, when waking up in the morning, we perceive our waking state as the exact opposite of sleep, whereas in reality there is only a slight difference between the two states.

Generally, we are totally unconscious when we are asleep and ninety-five percent unconscious when we are awake. Therefore, when we reach sixty, it is possible to estimate that we have only been conscious for about two years.

Moreover, remember that we don't actually recognize the conscious field itself, since our experience is monopolized by the phenomena we perceive in the field, whether thoughts or objects of material perception, that are external to the envelope of our body.

This gives us a clearer idea of how narrow our experience of identification with objects of perception (thoughts, emotions, sensations through the senses) really is within our existence. In the *Ocean of Certainty*, the narrow consciousness is compared to the space of a needle's eye of the ordinary man, while for an enlightened being it is like the limitless space.

Before continuing, it is important to remember that all the themes covered in this book illustrate different moments of our daily life. These are all interdependent and in interaction with each other.

It is impossible to consider sleep-related problems, or difficulties concentrating while meditating, without considering other times and activities in life, in which we are restless and involved. We can't improve our situation without considering the whole.

This is why I will now talk about the interactions between sleep and dreams using the following themes:

(1) Vigilance and alertness in daily life and quality of sleep

(2) Resolution and reduction of conflicts, conditions for good rest and sleep

(3) Sleep and rest

(4) Recapitulation

(5) Relaxation and improved rest and sleep

(6) Importance of breath in daily life

(7) How to nourish ourselves on a daily basis

VIGILANCE AND ALERTNESS IN DAILY LIFE AND QUALITY OF SLEEP

Whether we are still very trapped in duality or whether we are quite advanced on the path, for as long as there is ego grasping, everything is implicated in our existence.

The presence of restlessness, grasping, conflict or injustice in our daily lives, necessarily impacts our sleep and dreams, and our meditation.

Excessive emotional involvement on a daily basis creates an agitation that impacts the way we fall asleep, and the quality of our rest.

Our first duty is to be alert. Being alert and vigilant doesn't mean we become a moralizing despot. It means we apply a constant benevolent equanimous attention to everything we encounter without interruption.

The application of benevolent vigilance results from long-term observation which led us to conclude that it is better to apply a mediating vigilance than to fall into conflicts with the situations that manifest in every moment.

To establishing an alert vigilance we need to deeply and repeatedly wish for its presence and to preferably encourage this through regular meditation practice.

RESOLUTION AND REDUCTION OF CONFLICTS, CONDITIONS FOR GOOD REST AND SLEEP

All emotional and conflicting reactivity comes at a cost. We expend energy every time we stand in opposition with the immediate reality. This opposition to reality produces an accumulation of mental, emotional, and physical stress and tension. Sleep becomes difficult because tensions return when we try to fall asleep.

Alert vigilance allows us to be more aware in the present moment of our life conditions, circumstances, and context, and of the world around us. It also allows us to better perceive what's arising in our own mind. In this way, it prevents us from responding inappropriately to situations, and being carried away by mental and emotional contents.

Even if our progress is slow, through vigilant attention, we can avoid multiplying problems in our life and, thereby avoid increasing the tensions and fatigue that result from them. With vigilant attention, we waste less time dealing with problems that would otherwise arise.

Finally, vigilant attention allows us to better communicate with those around us. Over a lifetime, this can improve our life enormously. Vigilant attention allows us to perceive the more subtle signs in people's experience beyond what they express in words. Vigilant attention allows us to better identify people's needs expressed in their attitude and gestures, not only verbally.

Vigilant attention in daily life is associated with non-grasping, which can only be truly actualized through meditation practice.

When meditation is understood in this way—as developing the capacity to vigilance—it lets us be more present in our daily life, to grasp less and thus to better respond to situations.

Moreover, being vigilant in our daily lives reduces conflicts and saves us time and energy, which allows us to meditate better, be more peaceful when we fall asleep, have less troubled dreams, and rest more deeply.

It is not so much what is happening that we act on, but rather how we experience things. And how we experience what is happening outside or inside us depends on the state we are in.

Our state is continually conditioned. During our childhood, one, or even both of our parents, for reasons related to their own past, might have regularly worried and be prone to anxiety.

For us as babies, our parents necessarily had reasons to behave in the way they did. The problem is that as we age, we might still be perpetuating the same anxiety that we felt at twenty, fifteen, two years old, a baby, or even in our mother's womb.

Throughout our life, we might carry the weight of

an anxiety that was not, in fact, our own, but rather that of our mother and father, which distilled itself within us and continued for years.

While, at some point, our parents might have had objective reasons to be anxious, by maintaining the imprints of their anxiety, their behavior continues despite the absence of the original causes.

The causes of their anxiety remained active for no reason in the present moment, and may have possibly been projected into the future, for no reason either.

Their children can then create a future full of worry, limiting their present and everything they will undertake.

Once again, these should lead us to observation, alertness and vigilance. Observation allows us to see the interdependence of states and behaviors, and vigilance helps us to cut through negative chains to enter a more positive sense of existence.

SLEEP AND REST

Considering sleep and rest as necessarily connected is a mistake. We have all had the experience of waking up more tired than we were when we fell asleep. We also know that our dreams commonly reflect our conflicts and shortcomings and that they are not always restful.

Tensions at a mental, emotional, and physical level can be maintained even when we fall asleep. Some people even have heart problems while dreaming.

In the Buddhist context, sleep, mental opacity, and torpor, relate to the tendency of ignorance. Lucidity counters or cures the tendency of ignorance.

Becoming lucid in the phase of sleep without dreams, as well as in the dream phase, is the object of a Nidra yoga, a particular practice included in the *Six Yoga of Naropa* practices[45].

Let's take the example of three windowpanes, one of which is totally black, another frosted, and a third one just a little dirty. All these windowpanes are opaque in different degrees and prevent us from seeing what is outside. They also limit our experience of space which stops at their surface.

In the same way, we believe that we are aware of what we perceive up to the opaque windowpane, because our limited references are what we are used to.

If we wake up from a dream and remember it, it should lead us to conclude that there is something else that exists beyond the opaque windowpane of our unconscious, beyond the unconsciousness of our sleep, and beyond the enormous lack of awareness that exists when we are awake. Our lack of awareness during the waking state results in us grasping at the appearance of phenomena, in the same way that our perception is limited to the surface of an opaque window. We stop at the surface, thinking that this is what we should know, and that there is nothing else.

What traps us in the unconscious is the association we make of a name and an appearance (a form). Conceptual grasping happens through our sense perceptions. Conceptual grasping has us confusing knowing with experiencing and understanding.

---

45 The "*Six Yoga Practices of Naropa*" are: Yoga of psychic heat, Illusory body, Dream state, Clear light, Bardo, Transference of consciousness. See, "Le Yoga tibétain et les doctrines secrètes", Adrien Maisonneuve, 1948.
In English, see, "*The Six Yogas of Naropa: Tsongkhapa's Commentary Entitled A Book of Three Inspirations: A Treatise on the Stages of Training in the Profound Path of Naro's Six Dharmas*", 2005

To know the surface or the appearance of something, such as a windowpane, is not experiencing and understanding it. Things are not in their name or their appearance. Moreover, appearances prevent us from seeing the uncompounded reality that lies beyond.

If we don't train our consciousness to go beyond the border of what we know, we only know the appearances of awareness.

Most people do not remember their dreams. And when they remember them, they nevertheless continue to think that most of the time they are not dreaming.

For many of us, dreams are uninteresting, and can even be disturbing. Yet preventing someone from sleeping and dreaming leads to hallucinations and madness. We should therefore be grateful to our mind for generating dreams and thus allowing us, despite duality, not to mentally sink.

Dreams support and demonstrate our evolution. Dreams are the source of our creativity. Being unconsciousness of our dreams is an additional manifestation of the distance that separates us into two parts. These two parts should recognize each other as having essential roles within a unitary sense of self.

Before falling asleep, we rarely take the time to become aware of our tensions. Yet, tensions dissolve through us becoming aware of them. Becoming aware of our tensions doesn't means rejecting them, nor following them, or being unaware of them.

Before sleep, we lie down to recapitulate the emotions and conflicts that have generated tensions. We don't do that to rehash the past events and maintain them, quite the contrary. Conflicts and emotions generate tensions. Through ignorance, we fall asleep before considering the different aspects of our tensions. We cover up our conflicts and emotions, keeping them inside us without bringing them to light.

We thus fall asleep like a sack, a full sack which one day will burst at its seams. This isn't wise because our ignorance contributes to what will tomorrow encumber our present.

This is how, sooner or later, accumulated tensions, unresolved problems, and lack of integration of what has happened to us, turns into rumination, and prevent us from sleeping and resting.

Then, our level of agitation increases and our difficulties in responding appropriately to requests pile up in our daily life. Our various interactions amplify the consequences of our stress such as, for example, taking sedative tablets, or drugs to compensate and cope with our frustration and discomfort. By recognizing the above points, we can define and adopt a few useful principles and implement some easy practices to use on a daily basis.

To begin with, people who are agitated always give the reason that they lack time to practice when it would be good for them. They claim to have many things to do, many obligations! In fact, changing our habits is difficult, because habits have become another domain of ego extension (See, *Domain of ego extension*, page 25).

If we correctly implement the different means recommended, this will free up time and energy. First, we need to genuinely commit to viewing all the moments of our daily lives and the way we live them as clearly interdependent. We must constantly remember to do so.

Second, our consideration for the interdependent nature of things must be coupled with a firm commitment to alert vigilance. We settle into a relaxed and focused state, by repeatedly mentally developing a clear, simple, and positive aspiration to remember to be alert and vigilant[46].

Third, one doesn't become alert without training. The only systematic training in alertness is what is traditionally called "Shine"[47], the practice of concentration. It is also possible to actualize the tactile sensation as a support for attention and as a reminder.

THE PRACTICE OF RECAPITULATION

A fourth practice that is useful to implement is that of recapitulation. Recapitulation is a process leading to actualization, through the contemplation of past impressions and present situations, gradually including the principle of attention to the three spheres.

This practice consists of remaining aware of the three spheres (inside/me, outside/other, division/grasping) in each moment of our life, during the day, while we dream, and when we actualize memories in order to free ourselves from their imprints.

---

46 It is helpful to be guided in the process of being alert and vigilant. It is also possible to implement it alone. The aspiration to remember can be associated with a daily, simple, and repetitive act such as, for example, opening or closing a door.

47 Again, Shine or "zhinay": "shi" means tranquil, calming, "ne" means abiding. We attain calm abiding by first using a support of attention, either an external support, or the support of the breath.

As much as possible, the three spheres are perceived simultaneously from the field of awareness so to speak. Ultimately, what we perceive as separated in three distinctive spheres appear as existing within an undivided field.

When we practice recapitulation, we simultaneously perceive the suffering we have experienced, the self who has experienced such suffering, as well as the conflicting reaction that has arisen from it. We thus become aware of the three spheres that normally form negative imprints.

At the end of the day, before going to bed, we dedicate five to ten minutes, to recall situations that occurred during the day like in a freeze frame way. We start with the most recent scene, then go back replaying ten to fifteen scenes until we recall waking up at the beginning of that day.

We move fluidly from one scene to another, without looking for anything in particular. In each scene, we pay attention to the three spheres:

(1) The context, and the situation, what happens in it, what is outside.

(2) The interior space, what happens within us; our thoughts, feelings, emotions, and sensations.

(3) The overall sensation in our body, and our body posture, the limit between the previous two, me and other.

I do not recommend going back systematically to the actual conflicts we experienced during the day, nor to reflect, nor to moralize the recapitulation practice by updating moments when we have behaved in an inappropriate way. We are just there. We remember this in everyday situations and are simply present to the three spheres. We thus create a system that supports the establishment of a common thread of attention in our lives. Seeing what is right and wrong will naturally occur as our mind progressively reveals itself.

The recapitulation doesn't take long, we briefly revisit daily situations, without making the mistake of focusing our attention, exclusively on conflicts or problems. We contemplate with equality, pleasant, unpleasant, and neutral moments, following a meditative mindset, which means without grasping anything: just being aware.

To avoid other sources of restlessness before going to sleep we eat lightly, in small quantities, and leave a period of time between our last meal and bedtime.

We also identify the signs indicating the approach of a sleep cycle—yawning, the urge to stretch, watery eyes, heavy eyelids—without waiting to go to bed.

RELAXATION AND IMPROVED REST AND SLEEP

Fifth, comes the time to implement a relaxation practice. Before falling asleep we consciously relax our body through attention to the body, making an aspiration and paying attention to our breathing.

When we relax at a physical, emotional, and mental level before falling asleep, we enter into a deeper, truly restorative rest and, in the long term, we can rest better while sleeping less.

A practice of deep relaxation is one of the best things to engage in and implement over time.

We ritualize the practice of a relaxation protocol to which we have been introduced. By following a structured relaxation process, we avoid being drawn into the problems and difficulties linked to all our activities or concerns.

Before going to bed, without necessarily engaging in elaborated practices, a seated breathing practice can also be done. For example, we can take several deep breaths and then, after a long exhalation, we inhale for 4 to 6 seconds, we then suspend our breath for the same duration, and then we expire for the same time, 4 to 6 seconds. Then we remain still and empty of breath for the same duration,

This breathing technique channels our attention, it facilitates gas exchange, improves oxygenation and digestion. It can be enough if we practice it regularly every day.

Of course, people who practice yoga will find the above very basic and succinct. But this technique is accessible to everyone with no risk involved.

Still, as customary, I encourage you to find a qualified teacher to introduce you directly to the practices in this book, before implementing them.

Good food hygiene and abstinence from alcoholic beverages can improve snoring problems while asleep. Sometimes, when apnea isn't too serious, a healthy diet can solve it. Practices like cleaning our nose and using proper breathing practices can help as well.

The points that are described here should not be considered as solutions to specific problems that are serious. Although these practices can clearly produce good results, we should see them as elements of a whole way of living.

This whole way of living stems from a clear vision that all the moments of our daily life are interdependent and have consequences. Experiencing breathing difficulties, insomnia, or stress are all consequences.

When we see each one of our problems separately, we can still apply punctual remedies. But punctual remedies will never replace a mindset that has us include the meaning of our existence and relies on different means to live a wholesome life.

When we have experienced very disturbing events, and we suffer from insomnia because of our trauma, we might not succeed when we try to sleep. We go back to the destabilizing event and ruminate on it, while also trying to reject it. This pattern creates the ideal conditions for difficulties to take root.

We might then need some external support and appropriate interventions that take our specific circumstances into account. Seeking external help doesn't mean we are passive. We still implement ways to feel better in our life. We put things in place to improve our state of being, for example, relaxation practices, attending teaching, etc. We shouldn't limit ourselves to returning to the state we were in prior to receiving counseling support. These earlier states won't necessarily keep us in a balanced psycho-physical state.

Although sleep seems essential, and sleeping tablets can sometimes be useful, they don't solve our problems. Therefore, in order to return to natural rest and sleep, we should get the help we need rather than limiting ourselves to the use of chemical substances.

IMPORTANCE OF BREATH IN DAILY LIFE

As we noted earlier breathing is another way to nourish ourselves. While we can survive without solid food for several days, it is difficult to stop breathing for more than a few minutes. And not breathing for more than a few minutes requires serious training.

Despite the vital importance of our breathing, we pay little attention to it. Between our first breath, at birth, and our last sigh, we only pay interest to breathing when we lack it.

Yet breathing is the Ariadne's thread of our existence, a stable point we can connect with instead of being carried away by all that takes us away from the liveliness of the moment.

To breath is to stay alive. When daily events disturb us, through the influence of our emotions, our very first unconscious reaction is to breath in, and then block our breath, before exhaling a little, only by necessity. This conditioned response is just one aspect of the process of becoming tense that disturbs our dualistic mind, our emotions, and our body.

This is why it is important to pay more attention to our breathing. The oxygenation of our tissues, of our body, the proper functioning of our organs, our metabolism, our digestion, our circulation, our blood purification, and our energy, all depend on our breathing.

Of course, yoga practitioners already know this. However, without using complicated techniques, we can consider our breath in two aspects. The first is the role of breath in our physiology, and how we function as individuals. This aspect includes our mental, emotional, and physical dimensions.

The other aspect is the spiritual role of our breath as a support of attention in formal meditation, and the informal extension in daily life using breath as a support of attention.

Breath is so important to our life, we should give it as much attention as we give to what we are totally captivated by, someone or something. When we are really interested, we manifest it by giving it our full attention.

We should breathe consciously several times a day to sleep better and to have a clearer mind. When we are tense, emotional, or tired, we should breathe consciously.

When we breathe consciously, we slowly empty our lungs, then inhale for 3 seconds, and then exhale for 6 seconds. We do this regularly for a while. This is simple, easy, and accessible to everyone. Doing so while mentally counting the times of inhaling and exhaling helps channel our attention.

Once this simple training is mastered, we deepen this practice by emptying the lungs slowly, then inhaling for 3 seconds, suspending the breath for 3 seconds, exhaling for 6 seconds, then not breathing for 3 seconds. We begin by practicing this for 1 to 2 minutes then extend the duration of our conscious breathing practice and renew it regularly each day.

HOW TO NOURISH OURSELVES ON A DAILY BASIS

The food we eat should be regarded with respect. We need food in order to live this precious human life during which we can realize the nature of our own mind. That's why we dedicate our food to this purpose.

We dedicate our food to this purpose of realizing the nature of our own mind. Once we have digested and absorbed it, food becomes our flesh and blood. (Also, while we don't think about it, once we have ingested our food, it suddenly becomes part of us, part of "me", whereas a moment before it was "other".)

We should view food with equanimity, particularly when we eat meat in any form, for we ourselves will be a feast for the worms when we die. Within the manifestation, in all its forms, we can't dispute the fact that we can eat, as well as be eaten, and in this we feel how equal we are with others.

There are three forms of food. The coarsest type of food, which we eat, should be consumed in moderation and with attention.

The second type of food is more important. We receive it through our breath. We should pay more attention to it than to the food we eat.

The third is the nourishment of impressions. The nature of the mind absorbs the entire manifestation therein, we could say that awareness feeds on impressions. Progressing in the realization of the nature of the mind leads to full realization.

When it comes to solid or coarse food, we should be present, attentive, and happy while eating. When we are eating, we shouldn't mix our food with our troubles and tensions. Otherwise, we chew on troubles and tensions instead. This makes digesting our food as difficult as integrating what we reject in our day-to-day life.

When we eat, we should chew carefully, and properly taste and appreciate our food. In this way, we promote an easier digestion, facilitated by the gastric juices. We satisfy our psychological need to be full and better assimilate the nutrients through our contentment. Eating in this way is also an ecological measure since it saves food at the same time that it saves energy lost through difficult digestion.

We start each meal with raw vegetables and then take cooked food. If we eat meat, we take only a little. Of course, we strive to eat healthy, fresh, seasonal, food that is ideally locally sourced. It is better to absorb a variety of food. It is easier to digest one dish per meal and to vary the choice of foods from meal to meal.

These principles are simple and easy to implement. Of course, there are many principles of health and many competent specialists in this field. The principles mentioned here are based on common sense. They can be adapted according to specific needs.

Taking action, and fulfilment

At the end of life, what we didn't accomplish can make our grieving process difficult. Words we should have said but didn't give; a regret that hasn't led us to act in a fair and just way; inappropriate behavior that didn't result in repair; unfinished business; can all weigh heavily upon us.

The same happens for each day spent which ends with a thought like, "I should have, I could have, it would have been good to, I forgot to," etc."

However, being present and attentive is enough to respond to the needs of each day. We consciously list the needs of the day according to a hierarchy in terms of importance and urgency. When we do so, we base our daily life on accomplishment rather than failure at achieving anything.

Our capacity to accomplish our objectives is blocked by the negative aspects of the Karma tendency, which manifests as procrastination and a discontinuity in the flow of our mental activity.

It is extremely important in daily life that we face up to the situations we encounter and actively achieve the best possible outcomes. When we fail to keep up with the demands of life and fall into inaction (even when we are given the support we need), we accumulate feelings of incompetence or inadequacy which sets in motion a vicious cycle of failure and inaction. Then in order to realize anything of significance, greater efforts are required over longer periods of time.

In everyday life, everything our ego does is based on the goal of being recognized. This begins in childhood when we take our first steps, say our first words, and keep ourselves clean, in line with our parents' expectations. Our parents' pleasure or dissatisfaction depends upon what we accomplish or fail to do.

A whole system of "reward and recognition" is organized around conforming, or not, to what others expect of us. It begins with our parents. It is then driven further by everyone in a position of authority for us, those whose attention we seek to gain or avoid. This is to confirm an illusory sense of existing.

The purpose here is not to elaborate all the aspects of this system. Rather, I'll just say a few words about how to orient our activities positively in the direction of fulfillment.

Among all our activities, physical and intellectual activities should be balanced. Neuroscientists acknowledge the benefits of such a balance. I have observed for a long time that alternating physical and intellectual activities during the day promotes creativity, helps us to achieve our tasks, and gives us a feeling of accomplishment. By alternating physical and intellectual activities, we approach tasks or situations with increased enthusiasm.

When I work with people who tend to procrastinate and feel incapacitated, I recommend them to list specific objectives, even the most ordinary, for the following day or for the week ahead. And then, I ask them to cross out what they have achieved in each day. This is very useful.

People who have difficulties accomplishing and completing their projects, tend to compare themselves with others in a demeaning way and they often suffer from self-doubt. If we have this tendency, it is important to set close objectives and act on an everyday basis instead of indulging in rumination about feelings of incapacity.

Often in couples' life, one of the partners blocks the projects of the other, whether intentionally or not. If we block our partner's expression or projects, it can have many consequences. Our partner will certainly remember the obstructions.

In couples' life, the way in which we experience various impediments to our individual projects can resemble and reverberate with what happened in our childhood.

Children will remember if they were supported or thwarted in different projects they wanted to pursue. They always remember if they were encouraged or discouraged. They remember the past even more strongly when they have been prevented from expressing themselves through engaging in their projects.

If during our childhood, we encountered hinderances from others in our projects, or in our need to express ourselves, later on there is a likelihood that this pattern will be repeated within the dynamic of our couple, bringing difficulties to the relationship.

In the context of working with couples, I have noticed how difficulties within their relationships come from a poorly shared sexuality. This problem is not easy to solve but it is essential to invite everyone to take it into account. Being opened to talk about our sexuality would generate more harmonious relationships.

Whether in a lay life, or in a monastic framework, many cases of power inequality and abuse have demonstrated the difficulty of managing sexuality in a balanced way. This is linked to the topic of pure and impure, which we shouldn't ignore in a spiritual framework.

The dynamic of accomplishment manifests itself through volitions, the willpower of the individual. Through our dreams, the dynamic of accomplishment offers us the opportunity to realize the nondual emptiness of our mind and phenomena. This is the pinnacle of achievement.

But throughout our lives, and on a daily basis, this base of volitions, our will is directly linked to our sexuality. Our volition is also related to all forms of creativity, how we express ourselves, our various, projects, activities, and their fulfillment.

As soon as one of these domains of activity is blocked or interrupted, it greatly affects our appetite for living, our ability to accomplish things, or even just getting up in the morning. As a result, we become agitated, or depressed, or aggressive.

Once we are engaged on the spiritual path, we see how everything is interdependent, every moment, every circumstance, and all daily actions. We see how everything serves the purpose of achieving fulfillment.

People who are sick can choose to receive treatment for their illness. Alternatively, they may consider their life as a whole, by not only receiving treatment but by taking care of their emotional state, their mental health, as well as their body. Similarly, when we complete our daily actions to the best of our abilities, we rest better, because we have no regrets.

Isn't it wonderful to consider each moment as an opportunity to see the nature of our mind, which produces and perceives the manifestation, and to use each circumstance and the presence of every appearance to realize its nature.

Daily reminders
- Make a list of the goals for the day, and for the week
- Create a hierarchy of our objectives in terms of urgency and importance
- Define how we will achieve them
- Prioritize and classify each task
- Test and taste each experience
- Be aware of what we accomplish

Grief and separation

Fulfillment naturally brings with it the concept of grief. As I said before, what we have wished for, but failed to accomplish in life often weighs most heavily at the time of our death. The same heaviness can happen in our daily life.

We need to realize that many of our activities are only compensations or attempts to repair past frustrations. Consequently, most of our actions aren't choices consciously driven by what's happening in the present moment, nor by an awareness of who we are in the present. As most of our actions are determined by the past, how can they give us a true sense of accomplishment?

What arises in the moment is beyond rejection or acceptance. In order to grieve what no longer is, the past, we need to see and sense what appears in the present moment, as it is.

When we look at dictionary definitions of the words, bereavement, mourning, grief, and grieving process, they generally associate these experiences with loss, sadness, suffering and pain. But this doesn't have to be the case.

The definitions of these words usually link them to dying and death, and these usually implies suffering. We don't read about how such losses can be positive. However, we can initiate a process of integrating a person's death into the dynamic of life. Loss is an opportunity to moves on to novelty, to give way to life, just as, through their decay, fruits release new seeds, which bodes well for the future.

Why does it bode well? Because when self-centeredness decreases or ceases, attachment also ceases. The decrease of attachment gives way to love. This love is free of expectation and full of consideration for others. It's like we become heir to our deceased (heir of their conditionings, qualities, and lineage) and carry them within our own life from one moment to the next.

Dictionary definitions of grief also often associate the meaning of the word with resignation. We resign ourselves to a loss. But resignation is a way of avoiding grief. Instead of accepting the inevitability of death, we grudgingly let go, out of attachment, with great reluctance and pain, even resentment.

Once we let go of the past, of what we have moved through, then we start carrying our accumulated wisdom. This wisdom is not composed of regrets, it is totally linked to being truly present, in this moment. In each new moment, we are able to look at the past without identifying ourselves with it. Only then, can we speak of wisdom because awareness is no longer constrained or enslaved by a past that no longer exists.

Through discriminating wisdom, we open ourselves to altruism. We naturally let go of our many objects of attachments (our body, our possessions, and loved ones, what we believe we own). The energy of desire-attachment is rooted in duality. Desire-attachment is selfish and egocentric. Our ego mistakes attachment for love. As we depend on an other—who is the object of our attachment—when we are separated from our object of attachment, we no longer know who we are. We feel lost and disoriented.

When someone close to us dies, this threatens our very existence. It threatens the illusion of unity our ego likes to entertain through possessing people and the things we consider as our own. The suffering we experience is egocentric. The other, the relative or friend who died, knew our story, called us by our name. He or she was the witness of our life, the proof of our existence, we could read it in his or her eyes, etc. And this should end? "No ! How could this happen?" Our ego refuses to leave the bonds of attachment.

Obviously, it is hard for us to admit our egocentrism when we find ourselves in the situation of having lost someone. Unconsciously, the function of the objects of attachment—whatever they are, people or material possessions—is to reassure us that we exist.

Our objects of dependency often have a reassuring function. As soon as an object of attachment is lost, its dependency function appears. We are not really aware of its function before it disappeared, since we take our world as it is for granted. Like a turtle deprived of its shell, we start craving the object we depend on, and feel upset to no longer have it.

Why does this happen? Why are we always surprised when someone disappears, when present tense has become past tense? Why do we postpone telling people that we love them? Why do we let conflicts linger? Why do we always try to keep what feels good to ourselves?

We are undoubtably afraid of change. Perhaps we are crippled with habits. It's quite possible we have a habit of gaining comfort by regretting. At least regrets let us know we're still alive. Or do we simply lack courage? We lack the courage to change our habits, to be daring, to face truth, and cope with life and death.

Once we truly become aware of our limits, everything can change. We can stop viewing our limits as defects and start accepting them as characteristics. We then become aware that pure awareness—the awareness we are—perceives these characteristics and is therefore *beyond* them.

We need to experience and feel what we have thought of as defects—our fears, our lack of courage, our incapacity. We also need to feel a benevolent attention for ourselves, the "me", (myself), with which we have identified. It's only through presence and love that we give way, and dissolve into, who we really are.

In this way, our encounters with death, finitude, and suffering, are useful, as they contribute to a state of presence, and benevolent attention, which go hand in hand with equanimity.

Our psychic continuum is entirely composed of a stream of events functioning as causes and results, which we grasp as a unit, calling it me-myself. We must put an end to this causal chain of events.

Freeing ourselves from the causal reality requires a benevolent compassion for others. We are drawn to support people who are sick, people who are dying, people in pain. But we also respond with compassion to the inherent suffering of who we are. For as long as the imprint of self and others hasn't dissolved, we embrace the suffering of all beings, others, as well as our own. We are then able to express benevolence and hear distress without needing to prevent, stimulate or run away from its expression.

When we lack courage, we make do without courage. What has limited our capacity to share the depths of our suffering is a lack of presence and love. When presence and love have fully ripened, nothing can ever be missing.

Conclusion

My goal in in this book was to point out the various difficulties and challenges we encounter in daily life and how to work with them. This book offers different ways to reflect and orient our mind that are conducive [to wellbeing and liberation].

You may have gained some clarity about the themes that resonated with you. Perhaps you agreed with some of the ideas developed in this book and have decided to implement one, or several of the practices described.

This is what matters, making a start, taking action, feeling how each moment is new in that it was never lived before. We respect our precious human rebirth by not letting the past enslave us, even if it was difficult.

We don't only believe, we practice. We become a practitioner of our life in order to accomplish the welfare of others and our own wellbeing.

We set specific goals. We establish a hierarchy within them. Our ultimate goal and relative goals are used to define precise steps towards the final objective we have set for ourselves.

We also need to define precise methods to achieve our goals now and tomorrow. We resist ego's seductive games that keep us confined within the barriers of our habits and stop us.

We overcome ego pleasing intentions that produce nothing. Instead, we define and accomplish [altruistic] goals. Hell is paved with good intentions that lead nowhere and impoverish our life instead of enriching it.

Every day, we check that our immediate goals have been reached. We also check that we have taken the necessary steps towards our ultimate goal. We move forward in a regular, precise, and systematic way. We cultivate fulfillment.

In this book, I have given some directions, some elements for reflection, and some orientations using long and well tested methods. Most of the practices described require additional instructions and personal guidance from a qualified teacher. Their presentation here is not exhaustive. Rather it is a set of ideas to which you can refer. I hope that it is of benefit to some readers. If there are any mistakes, these are the sole responsibility of the author.

"May all beings achieve happiness and peace."

Acknowledgements

To Arnaud, for his dedicated work for the benefit of all. To Marie, for her help, her suggestions, and corrections. To Pascal, whose perseverance has never wavered. To Danielle, for her advice, her suggestions, and corrections and for the activity she offers. To Sadia, for the help and support she has given me. To Michèle, who works hard at communicating with all of my students. And finally, to all of my students who, from near or far, helped me with their presence. In particular, to all those who devote themselves to the welfare of others, by running workshops, and by accompanying people in their suffering.

For this english version, I would like to express all my gratefulness to Marie and Peter for their translation of this text, making it accessible now for the english audience

Dedication

I dedicate this book to Lama Teunsang. For all who know him, he is the greatest example of how to incarnate the path of the six transcendent virtues: perseverance, discipline, generosity, courage, concentration, and wisdom. He has never ceased to transmit these virtues throughout his life.

To my children, David, Arnaud, and Emmanuelle, and to Michèle, their mother. They have sacrificed a great deal because of my activities.

And to their partners: Blandine, Céline and Jérôme.

To my grandchildren: Victor and Jeanne, Lucas and Zoé, Anatole and Ambre.

I have been blessed with a lot of good luck, or good karma, to have met them, and I wish them happiness, love and peace.

I am grateful for all those who have practiced with me. I thank them for the trust they have placed in me. They have taught me a lot. They remain present [in my heart] through the help they provide in a variety of ways. I wish all of them happiness and fulfillment.

Alain

Publishing finished
in march 2023 by Pulsio
Publisher Number: 4021
Legal Deposit: march 2023
Printed in Bulgaria